Kundalini

The Mother of the Universe

The Mystery of Piercing
the Six Chakras

By

Rishi Singh Gherwal

Copyrighted and Published
by Author

1930

Santa Barbara Calif. U. S. A.

P. O. Box 533

LA EPOCA
The Spanish Printers
San Antonio, Texas

Printing Statement:

Due to the very old age and scarcity of this book, many of the pages may be hard to read due to the blurring of the original text, possible missing pages, missing text and other issues beyond our control.

Because this is such an important and rare work, we believe it is best to reproduce this book regardless of its original condition.

Thank you for your understanding.

On page 65, 8th line from top, line repeated which
should read:
"yam into anritam, which is called destrue-"

To My Mother

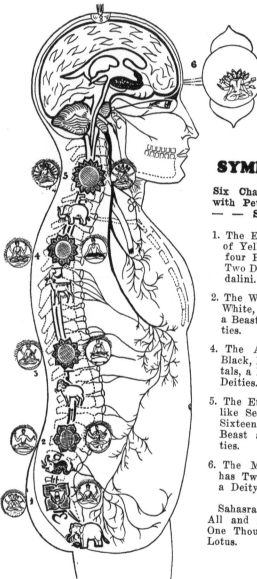

SYMBOLICAL

Six Chakras of Yoga with Petals and Deity — — Symbols — —

1. The Earth Chakra is of Yellow color, has four Petals, a Beast, Two Deities and Kundalini.

2. The Water Chakra is White, has Six Petals, a Beast and Two Deities.

4. The Air Chakra is Black, has Twelve Petals, a Beast and Two Deities.

5. The Ether Chakra is like Sea Water, has Sixteen Petals, a Beast and Two Deities.

6. The Mental Chakra has Two Petals and a Deity.

Sahasrara is Above All and is called, the One Thousand Petalled Lotus.

THE MOTHER OF THE UNIVERSE
The Book of Kundalini Contains:

In ordering Book write to
Rishi S. Gherwal or J. Falkenstein.

P. O. Box 533   Santa Barbara, Calif.
U. S. A.

TO THE KUNDALINI – THE MOTHER OF THE UNIVERSE.

"What Yogis now, what Rishis of old,
The greatness of that Mother hath told,
Who from her own breast gave birth
To the sky and to the earth.

Thou hung the Heavens in empty space,
And holds the earth in its place,
Thou made and lighted up the sun
To stay and shine this earth upon.

Thy power transcendent, since their birth
Asunder holds the heaven and earth,
As chariot wheels are kept apart
By axles made thru workman's art.

In Shakti, who with thee can vie,
Thou fills the earth, the air, the sky;
Thy presence, unperceived, extends
Beyond the world's remotest ends.

A million earths, if such there be,
A million skies fall short of thee;
A billion suns can not out shine
The effulgence of thy light divine.

The worlds, which mortals boundless deem
To thee but as a handfull seem.
Mother, Thou art without a peer.
On earth, or in yonder heavenly sphere.

VI

Thee, God, such matchless powers adorn
That thou without a foe was born.
Thou art the Lord of Lords,
Adored by Men—reverred by Gods.

The circling times which wear away,
All else, to thee can not decay;
Thou shinest on in youthful force,
While countless Yugas run their course.

Unvexed by cares, or fears, or strife,
In bliss serene flow on thy life,
With faith we claim thine aid divine,
As thou art Mother, and we are thine.

An old Hindu prayer. The metrical translation from the Sanskrit writers, by Mr. J.
Muir, with modifications by author.

My sincere thanks to every author and
publisher, here quoted in my book and I also
want to add my thanks to Irene Ward, Grace
Curtis and Clare McKinney for their unceasing efforts to help me bring it out in
three weeks.

If all great men were good and all good men would write a book this world would be made better by their activities.

Rishi Gherwal's books are observations of nature and nature is God's "Master-piece". They are historical records of true facts of the Hindu books on philosophy, and are like a visit to that old ancient Temple of Mathra.

His manner of teaching and writing inspires us with the knowledge of ourselves, to be the same as the Universal Brotherhood—, Self of the Universe, with God's poise and sense of mastery.

His books give us the blessed assurance that we no longer need to travel to get wisdom. Study TRUTH and absorb its teachings, and the world will come to you, as it has to him.

May Peace be Unto him, together with a benediction of love, with our blessings.

Dr. and Mrs. J. D. Ward.

INTRODUCTION

KUNDALINI, THE MOTHER OF
THE UNIVERSE.

"O God of Gods, Thou art a
Father, Mother, kinsman, friend.
Knowledge, riches, all—I find in Thee,
All good Thy being comprehends."

India is the mysterious land chosen as her
own by Kundalini, The Mother of the Universe. What we read in old histories and
Holy Bibles, and the records, can be seen
there today.

In India there are Yogis who perform
such marvelous feats that Doctors, Scientists and Chemists are unable to solve them,
and I may say, are unable to understand
them. For instance, such feats, as lying
down upon blazing logs of fire; walking
over red hot fire that has been especially pre-
pared by burning ten tons of wood,—twenty
men walked over this without a burn—not
even a hair on their feet; also feats of levitation, walking on water, etc., equally as as-
tonishing.

Yogi Haridas, at Lahore, willingly permitted himself to be buried alive for forty days under fifteen feet of earth. After that length of time, he was taken out as normal as ever. Such as that, and standing on one leg for years; head buried in the earth with both legs up in the air for days; living without food for forty years,—these and many other things can be seen in India today.

Any one wishing to read further about this may obtain the author's booklet entitled: "Marvelous feats performed by Yogis through Yoga."

I have received many letters asking: "How can that be done?" The answer is, they always do this through the Kundalini (The Divine Mother) by awakening her from her sleep, for then any one can have supernatural power — this is her gift with unfoldment.

"Kundalini the Giver of Health"; "Kundalini the Giver of Wealth"; "Kundalini the Giver of Joy and Happiness"; "Kundalini the Giver of Faith"; "Kundalini the Giver of Bliss, Life, and Powers."

By awakening her, seeming miracles can be performed by men and women. The resurrection came as a living faith; see "The Great Masters of the Himalayas" — by the author.

10

The Kundalini is always back of all powers and feats of seeming miracles. She is
the All in All.

Swami Vivekananda says: "Whenever
there is any manifestation of what is ordinarily called supernatural power or wisdom,
there must have been a little (control over
the) current of Kundalini which found its
way into the Sushumna. Only, in the vast
majority of such cases of supernaturalism,
they ignorantly stumble on some practice
which set free, (and made them conscious
of) a minute portion, (of the control) of
the coiled up Kundalini."

The Kundalini (Divine Mother), always
keeps for herself a chosen country, in which
her higher wisdom is preserved from all
dangers.

That land is India. When she wanted to
see the play of helplessness, weakness and ignorance of the world, she chose that land.
When the Kundalini again wants to raise
up from ignorance to Mighty Wisdom, and
a Blissful state, she chooses India again, for
the purpose of raising India once more to
the highest of Pure Wisdom.

In ages past the greatest Avatars, of India–Sri Rama Chandar, Ram Sri, Sri Krish-

na, King Janak, Yajuvalkya, Guru Nanik, Buddha and countless others. The present day we have Saint Mahatma Gandhi.

Why does the Kundalini choose India? To perfect her being and for the purpose of perfecting harmony. That only can save the world from misery of selfishness and hate.

Only India can find harmony. That harmony is by change of heart. Such change and harmony comes by Yoga. Yoga can and will change the mind, heart, and action; this change is from within; not from without.

Not by politics nor by creeds but by the realization of the Goddess Kundalini, remodeling life by pure Wisdom—not by knowledge. This Divine Harmony is not alone for suffering humanity, but for even the smallest insects, animals, etc.

That change of heart, that Blessed Harmony, the son of Mother India, Mahatma Gandhi, has shown the world.

Have I lost my sense of understanding to make a statement about India? Not so, I am conscious and seeing with clear vision. The India that has kept true to Spirituality, in the past ages against all storms of material opposition, is now the chosen land of Mother Kundalini.

I sincerely trust that my many friends and seekers of Truth, who are looking to California for the future Spiritual Teacher of the world, will not be hurt by the above statement. Truth is Truth, although it hurts many, many times.

"Lo, in the East this Wisdom's showering Light
Adorable, hath sprung from out the night;
Now may the Dawns, heaven daughters, spread
Shining afar, a path for man to tread."

"If I were to look over the whole world to find out the country most richly endowed with all the wealth, power and beauty that nature can bestow, in some parts a very paradise on earth—I should point to India. If I were asked under what sky the human mind has most fully developed some of its choicest gifts, has most deeply pondered on the greatest problems of life, and has found solutions of some of them which well deserved the attention even of those who have studied Plato and Kant, I should point to India. If I were to ask myself from

13

what literature we, here in Europe, may draw the corrective which is most wanted in order to make our inner life more perfect, more universal, in fact more truly human, again I should point to India."

–MAX MULLER.

Pope Pius IX says:- "India alone has remained true to the heart of the spiritual motives. " (From Sir Woodroffe's book –"Is India Civilized?")

"THE YOGA AND ITS OBJECT"

Whenever we see or read of any miracles of supernatural power shown by human beings in India it is always done by Yoga.

What is this Yoga that gives such wonderful power, divine peace, longevity, etc.?

Yoga is the science of sciences, it is the way that leads to Godhood. "The Yoga we practice, is not for ourselves alone, but for humanity. Its object is not personal Mukti (liberation), although Mukti is a necessary condition of the Yoga, but the libration of the human race. It is not personal ananda (bliss), but the bringing down of the divine Ananda – Christ's Kingdom of Heaven, our Satyayuga upon the earth".—

—An excerpt from "The Yoga and Its Objects".

"Humanity is evolving. Yoga is the means of carrying that evolution forward with great and victorious rapidity", "Yogic Sadhan".

"The goal marked out for us is not to speculate about these things but to experience them. The call upon us is to grow into the image of God, to dwell in Him and with

Him and be a channel of His joy and might
and an instrument of His works. Purified
from all that is Asubha (evil), transfigured
in soul by His touch we have to act in the
world as dynamos of that divine electricity
and send it thrilling and radiating thru mankind, so that wherever one of us stands,
hundreds around may become full of His
light and force, full of God and full of Ananda (the bliss of the spirit). Churches,
orders, theologies, philosophies have failed
to save mankind because they have busied
themselves with intellectual creeds, dogmas,
rites and institutions, with achara sudhi and
darshana, as if these could save mankind,
and have neglected the one thing needful,
the power and purification of the soul. We
must go back to the one thing needful, take-
up again Christ's Gospel of the purity and
perfection of mankind, Mahomed's gospel
of perfect submission, self-surrender and
servitude of God, Chaitanya's gospel of
the perfect love and joy of God in man,
Ramkrishna's gospel of the unity of all
religions and the divinity of God in man,
and gathering all these streams into one
mighty river, one purifying and redeeming
Ganges, pour it over the death-in-life of a

materialistic humanity as Bhagiratha led down the Ganges and flooded with it the ashes of his fathers, so that there may be a resurrection of the soul in mankind and the Satya yuga for a while returns to the world. Nor is this the whole object of the Lila or the Yoga, the reason for which the Avatars descend is to raise up man again and again, developing in him a higher and ever higher-humanity, a greater and yet greater development of divine being, bringing more and more of heaven again and again upon the earth until our toil is done. Our work accomplished and Sachchidananda fulfilled in all even here, even in this material universe. Small is his work, even if he succeeds, who labours for his own salvation or the salvation of a few, infinitely great is he even if he fail or succeed only partially or for a season, who lives only to bring about peace of soul, joy, purity and perfection among all mankind.''

Exerpt from the ''Yoga and Its Objects'' by a Master.

LOCATION OF KUNDALINI

Every one has many bodies, but I will deal with only two at this time, the Sthula (gross body) and the Sukshma (the subtle body). These two bodies can be easily understood by every one. The gross body can be felt but the subtle body can reason, as every one has experienced in the dreaming state. What keeps these two bodies together? There are ten pranas; five are subtle and five are gross. The gross pranas are in the gross body and move thru the gross Nadis or nervous system. The subtle pranas are in the subtle body and move thru the subtle Nadis. These two pranas are connected about the heart which is the organ of sensation. When the poets and others felt that sensation, they called it Atma or God in the heart. The other connection of the pranas is between the heart and the navel, that is the mind. The subtle body has as many nerves as the gross body. The three main ones are the Ida, Pingala and Sushumana. The Ida Nerve is on the left side, the Pingala is on the right and between the two is Sushumana. The mouth of the Sushu-

mana is closed by the Goddess Kundalini as
she is sleeping at the door of the Sushumana.
The Kundalini is in the subtle body and remains there always, but part of her divine
energy is in the gross body and manifested
as Prana, Apana, Vyana, Samana and U-
dana. The Kundalini is the creator and the
sustainer of the universe. She is the All in
All.

The best authority on the Kundalini is
the Hatha Yoga Pradipika. It says: "The
Kundalini is sleeping, closing the door of the
Sushumana. She sleeps above the Kanda or
where the Nadis unite. She gives liberation
to the Yogi and bondage to fools. He who
knows her knows Yoga."

The location of the Kanda is 12 angulis
(or about 9 inches) above the anus and 3
inches long and 3 inches in breadth. It is the
shape of a bird's egg and covered with a soft
white piece of "cloth."

Great Rishi Yajnavalkya says the Kanda
is about the same location. All authorities
on Yoga give the location of the Kanda in
the lower part of the body above the anus;
and there is sleeping the Kundalini.

The Hatha Yoga Pradipika says further
about the Kanda and Kundalini: "Yogins

19

awake the Kundalini that is sleeping at the door of the Sushumana. Seated on the Vajrasan and taking hold of the ankles, Yogi should slowly beat the Kanda."

We read in the Sharada Tilaka about Kundalini: "We pray to the Paradevata united with Shiva, whose substance is the pure nectar or bliss, red like unto vermillion, the young flower of the hibiscus, the sunset sky, who having crept her way thru the mass of sound issuing from the clashing and dashing of the two winds in the midst of the Sushumana, rises to the brilliant energy which glitters with the lustre of ten million lightnings. May she the Kundalini, who quickly goes to and returns from Shiva, grant us the fruit of Yoga! She being awakened is the cow of plenty to Kaulas, and the Kalpa Creeper of all things desired for those who worship her."

The Kundalini is the support of all, the Yoga is the means to reach her.

WHAT IS THE KUNDALINI WHEN AWAKENED – WHAT THEN?

The Kundalini, when awakened, is the giver of all power, health, wealth and success. The Kundalini feeds the baby in the mother's womb. She fulfills our every desire. She is the All in All.

"I praise Tripura which is the treasure house of the race.

"The Kundalini, has three angles as well as three circles, and her Bhupura is three-lined. Her Mantra is three syllables, and she has three aspects. The Kundalini energy is also threefold in order that she may create the three Gods (Brahma, the Creator, or air; Vishnu, the Preserver, or water: Rudra, the Destroyer, or fire). Since she is triple everywhere, she is Tripura."

"O Mother of the Universe, those who praise you by the words, Mother, All in All, and Maya, will obtain all.

"There is nothing which can not be obtained on earth or in the Heavens, by Thy Grace."

This is as it should be, as the Kundalini is Power of Powers, Light of Lights, and All in All.

The Kundalini is Divine static and dynamic energy. The static energy (Kundalini), is sleeping at the Muladhara (Root Chakra); the dynamic energy of the Kundalini is all over the body as Prana, Apana, Samana, Vyana, and Udana. These five Vital breaths, or life forces, keep the body together. The duties of the five Pranas are as follows: Prana remains in the upper part of the body, and always moves upward; the Apana resides in the lower part of the body, or abdomen, and always flows downward; the Samana stays in the first section of the torso, digesting and distributing the food substances; the Vyana resides in the heart, and from there moves all over the body, its duty being the circulation of the blood; the Udana carries the Soul upward when the body dies.

These five Pranas stay in the grosser body. They are also in the finer or subtle body—the five finer breaths corresponding to the five grosser Pranas above described.

The Pranayama Yoga, the Mudra Yoga, and Dharana Yoga, are all for the control of the five Pranas and mind. Mind without Prana is like a bird without wings. The practice of the Mudras is to control the dynamic energy of the Kundalini, namely, Pra-

22

na, Apana, etc. The practice of Pranayama
is also to control the Prana, Apana, etc.—the
dynamic energy of the Kundalini, and with
it awaken the static energy of the Kundalini, which is sleeping at the Muladhara, or
root Chakra. When the five Pranas are controlled or made to stop at the desired place,
the Muladhara Chakra, or at the door of
the Sushumana, it will work like a spark to
the static energy of the Kundalini.

"When Prana and Apana are mixed, it
will naturally cause heat in the body; then
the body becomes light and powerful. This
extreme heat when felt by the Kundalini,
causes her to awaken from sleep. Then she
goes into the Sushumana." (From H. Y. P.)

The duty of the Yogin is to gather together or control the five Pranas—the life force
of the Kundalini—that the dynamic energy
of the Kundalini may be used to awaken the
static energy of it, as one Kundalini energy
will move the other energy.

When the Kundalini awakens or moves,
what then remains? What will become of
the Kundalini? She will go to the Six Chakras and also remain at her place. As steam
is converted from water by heat and again
returns to it, so rises the dynamic energy of

the Kundalini, which goes up to the different Chakras and returns again and again. While she will reach to the Sahasrara, still she will be at her home at the Muladhara Chakra.

The Kundalini power can only be known by Master Yogins, but some times even ordinary Yogins can see it, however not as clearly, as long as the inner eye is not open. When the Yogin has opened the inner eye, then he sees the different Chakras and the energy of the Kundalini, which is Life of Life, and Light of Lights.

The following Masterly and Scientific explanation of the Kundalini is by Prof. P. Mukhyopadhyaya, and was written for Arthur Avalon and brought out in his book.

"The Serpent Power," pp. 302–313.

I here acknowledge my thanks for the use of this explanation, and I wish that every student of Yoga would read "The Serpent Power." R. S. Gherwal.

"When you say that Kundali Shakti is the primordial Shakti at rest, I am led to think of an analogy (and it may be more than an analogy) in modern science. Cosmic energy in its physical aspect may be considered either as static or as dynamic, the former being a condition of equilibrium, the latter a condition of motion or change of relative position. Thus a material thing apparently at rest (there being no absolute rest except in pure Consciousness or Chit) should be regarded as energy or Shakti equilibrated, the various elements of it holding one another in check (or, as the mathematicians will say, the algebraic sum of the forces being zero). Of course, in any given case the equilibrium is relative rather than absolute. The important thing to note is this polarisation of Shakti into two forms—static and dynamic.

"In the tissues of a living body, again, the operative energy (whatever the nature of that may be, whether we believe in a special 'vital force' or not) polarises itself into two similar forms—anabolic and katabolic—one tending to change and the other to conserve the tissues, the actual condition of the tissues being simply the resultant of these two coexistent or concurrent activities.

"In the mind or experience also this polarisation or polarity is patent to reflection. In my own writings *I have constantly urged

*"Approaches to Truth", "The Patent Wonder", valuable presentments in modern terms of the ancient Vedantic teaching.

this polarity between pure Chit and the stress which is involved in it: there is a stress or Shakti developing the mind through an infinity of forms and changes; but all these forms and changes are known as involved in the pure and unbounded ether of awareness (Chidakasha). This analysis therefore exhibits the primordial Shakti in the same two polar forms as before—static and dynamic—and here the polarity is most fundamental and approaches absoluteness.

"Lastly, let us consider for one moment the atom of modern science. The chemical atom has ceased to be an atom (indivisible unit of matter). We have instead the electron theory. According to this, the so-called atom is a miniature universe very much like our own solar system. At the centre of this atomic system we have a charge of positive electricity round which a cloud of negative charges (called electrons) is supposed to revolve, just as myriads of planets and smaller bodies revolve round the sun. The positive and the negative charges hold each other in check, so that the atom is a condition of equilibrated energy, and does not therefore ordinarily break up, though it may possibly break up and set free its equilibrated store of energy, as probably it does in the emanations of the radium. What do we notice here? The same polarity of Shakti into a static and a dynamic partner—viz., the positive charge at rest at the centre, and the negative charges in motion round about the centre; a most suggestive analogy or illustration, perhaps, of the cosmic fact. The illustration may be carried into other domains of science and philosophy, but I may as well forbear going into details. For the present we may, I think, draw this important conclusion:

"Shakti, as manifesting itself in the universe, divides itself into two polar aspects—static and dynamic—which implies that you cannot have it in a dynamic form without at the same time having it in a corresponding static form, much like the poles of a magnet. In any given sphere of activity of force we must have, according to this cosmic principle, a static background—Shakti at rest or 'coiled', as the Tantras say.

"Before I proceed, let me point out what I conceive to be the fundamental significance of our Tantric and Pauranic Kali. This figure or Murti is both real and symbolic, as indeed every Murti in the so-called Hindu

27

mythology is. Now, the Divine Mother
Kali is a symbol of the cosmic truth just
explained. Sadashiva, on whose breast She
dances, nude and dark, is the static background of pure Chit, white and inert (Sha-
varupa), because pure Chit is in itself Sva-
prakasha (self manifest) and Nishkriya (actionless). At the same time, apart from and
beyond Consciousness there can be nothing
— no power or Shaki — hence the Divine
Mother stands on the bosom of the Divine
Father. The Mother Herself is all activity
and Gunamayi (in Her aspect as Prakriti
composed of the Gunas). Her nakedness
means that, though She encompasses all,
there is nothing to encompass Herself; her
darkness means that She is inscrutable,
Avang—manasagochara (beyond the reach
of thought and speech). Of course, this is
no partition of reality into two (there lies
the imperfection of the Sangkhya doctrine
of Purusha and Prakriti, which is otherwise
right), but merely polarisation in our
experience of an indivisible fact which is the
primordial (Adya) Shakti itself. Thus
Chit is also Shakti. Shiva is Shakti and
Shakti is Shiva, as the Tantras say. It
is Gunashraya (support of Gunas) as

well as Gunamaya (whose substance is Gunas); Nirguna (attributeless) as well as Saguna (with attribute), as said in a well-known passage of the Chandi.

"Your suggestive hint [2]makes the nature of the Kundali Shakti rather clear to me. You are quite right, perhaps, in saying that the cosmic Shakti is the Samashti (collectivity) in relation to which the Kundali in the bodies is only the Vyashti (individual): it is an illustration, a reproduction on a miniature scale, a microcosmic plan, of the whole. The law or principle of the whole—that of macrocosmic Shakti—should therefore be found in the Kundali. That law we have seen to be the law of polarisation into static-dynamic or potential-kinetic aspects. In the living body, therefore, there must be such polarisation. Now, the Kundali coiled three times and a half at the Muladhara is the indispensable and unfailing static background of the dynamic Shakti operative in the whole body, carrying on processes and working out changes. The body, therefore, may be compared to a magnet with two poles. The Muladhara is the static pole in relation to the rest of the body, which is dyna-

2 That Kundalini in the static Shakti.

mic; the working the body necessarily presupposes and finds such a static support, hence perhaps[3] the name Muladhara, the fundamental support. In one sense, the static Shakti at the Muladhara is necessarily coexistent with the creating and evolving Shakti of the body, because the dynamic aspect or pole can never be without its static counterpart. In another sense, it is the Shakti **left over** (you have yourself pointed this out, and the italics are yours), after the Prithivi — the last of the Bhutas — has been created, a magazine of power to be drawn upon and utilized for further activity, if there should arise any need for such. Taking the two senses together (yours as well as mine), Shakti at the Muladhara is both coexistent with every act of creation or manifestation and is the residual effect of such act—both cause and effect, in fact—an idea which, deeply looked into, shows no real contradiction. There is, in fact, what the physicist will describe as a cycle or circuit in action. Let us take the impregnated ovum—the earliest embryological stage of the living body. In it the Kunda-

3. Certainly.

li Shakti is already presented in its two polar aspects: the ovum, which the mother-element represents, one pole (possibly the static), and the spermatazoon, which is the father-element, represents the other (possibly the dynamic).[4] From their fusion proceed those processes which the biologist calls differentiation and integration; but in all this process of creation the cycle can be fairly easily traced. Shakti flows out of the germinal cell (fertilised ovum), seizes upon foreign matter, and assimilates it and thereby grows in bulk; divides and subdivides itself, and then again co-ordinates all its divided parts into one organic whole. Now in all this we have the cycle. Seizing upon foreign matter is an outwardly directed activity, assimilation is an inwardly directed activity or return current; cell division and multiplication is an outwardly directed operation, co-ordination is inwardly directed; [5] and so on. The force in the germ - cell is overflowing, but also continuously it is flowing back into itself, the two operations presupposing and sustaining each other, as in every circuit.

4. The process of fertilisation is dealt with in the Matrikabheda Tantra.
5. This outflow and inflow is a common Tantrik notion.

The given stock of force in the germ-cell, which is static so long as the fusion of the male and female elements does not take place in the womb, is the necessary starting-point of all creative activity; it is the primordial cause, therefore, in relation to the body — primordial as well as constantly given, unceasing. On the other hand, the reaction of every creative action, the return current or flowing back of every unfolding over flow, constantly renews this starting force, changes it without changing its general condition of relative equilibrium (and this is quite possible, as in the case of any material system); the force in the germ-cell may therefore be also regarded as a perpetual effect, something left over and set against the working forces of the body. Many apparently inconsistent ideas enter into this conception, and they have to be reconciled.

"1. We start with a force in the germ-cell which is statical at first (though, like a dicotyledon seed, or even a modern atom, it involves within itself both a statical and a dynamical pole; otherwise, from pure rest, involving no possibility of motion, no mottion could ever arise). Let this be the Kundali coiled.

"2. Then there is creative impulse arising out of it; this is motion out of rest. By this, the Kundali becomes partly static and partly dynamic, or ejects, so to say, a dynamic pole out of it in order to evolve the body, but remaining a static pole or background itself all along. In no part of the process has the Kundali really uncoiled itself altogether, or even curtailed its three coils and a half. Without this Muladhara Shakti remaining intact no evolution could be possible at all. It is the hinge upon which everything else turns.

"3. Each creative act again reacts on the Muladhara Shakti, so that such reaction, without disturbing the relative rest of the coiled Shakti, changes its volume or intensity, but does not curtail or add to the number of coils. For instance, every natural act of respiration reacts on the coiled Shakti at the Muladhara, but it does not commonly make much difference. But Pranayama powerfully reacts on it, so much so that it awakes the dormant power and sends it piercing through the centres. Now, the common description that the Kundali uncoils Herself then and goes up the Sushumna, leaving the Muladhara, should, I think, be admitted with caution. That static background can never be absolutely dispensed with. As you have yourself rightly observed, 'Shakti can never be depleted, but this is how to look at it'. Precisely; the Kundali, when powerfully worked upon by Yoga, sends forth an emanation or ejection in the likeness of Her own self (like the 'ethereal double' of the Theosophists and Spiritualists) which pierces through the various centres until it becomes blended, as you point out, with the Mahakundali of Shiva at the highest or seventh centre. Thus, while this' 'ethereal double' or self-ejection of the coiled power at the Muladhara ascends the Sushumna, the coiled power itself does not and need not stir from its place. It is like a spark given from an over saturated [6] electro-magnetic machine; or, rather, it is like the emanations of radium which do not sensibly detract from the energy contained in it. This last, perhaps, is the closest physical parallel of the case that we are trying to understand. As a well-known passage in the Upanishad has it, 'The whole (Purna) is subtracted from the whole, and yet the whole remains.' I think our present case

6. Overcharged.

34

comes very near to this. The Kundali at the
Muladhara is the whole primordial Shakti
in monad or germ or latency: that is why it
is coiled. The Kundali that mounts up the
Nadi is also the whole Shakti in a specially
dynamic form—an eject likeness of the Eternal Serpent. The result of the last fusion
(there are successive fusions in the various
centres also) in the Sahasrara is also the
whole, or Purna. This is how I look at it.
In this conception the permanent static
background is not really depleted, much less
is it dispensed with.

"4. When again I say that the volume
or intensity of the coiled power can be affected (though not its configuration and
relative equilibrium), I do not mean to
throw up the principle of conservation of
energy in relation to the Kundali, which is
the embodiment of all energy. It is merely
the conversion of static (potential) energy
into dynamic (kinetic) energy in part, the
sum remaining constant. As we have to
deal with infinities here, an exact physical
rendering of this principle is not to be ex-
pected. The Yogi therefore simply' 'awakens', and never creates Shakti. By the way,
the germ-cell which evolves the body does

not, according to modern biology, cease to be a germ-cell in any stage of the complicated process. The original germ-cell splits up into two: one half gradually develops itself into the body of a plant or animal—this is the somatic cell; the other half remains encased within the body practically unchanged, and is transmitted in the process of reproduction to the offspring—that is, the germ-plasm. Now, this germ-plasm is unbroken through the whole line of propagation. This is Weismann's doctrine of 'continuity of the germ-plasm,' which has been widely accepted, though it is but an hypothesis."

In a subsequent postscript the Professor wrote:

"1. Shakti being either static or dynamic, every dynamic form necessarily presupposes a static background. A purely dynamic activity (which is motion in its physical aspect) is impossible without a static support or ground (Adhara). Hence the philosophical doctrine of absolute motion or change, as taught by old Heraclitus and the Buddhists and by modern Bergson, is wrong; it is based neither upon correct logic nor upon clear intuition. The constitution of an atom reveals the static-dynamic polarisation of Shak ti; other and more complex forms of existence also do the same. In the living body this necessary static background is Muladhara, where Shakti is Kundali coiled. All the functional activity of the body, starting from the development of the germ-cell, is correlated to, and sustained by the Shakti concentrated at, the Muladhara. Cosmic creation, too, ending with the evolution of Prithivi Tattva (it is, however, an unending process in a different sense, and there perhaps Henry Bergson, who claims that the creative impulse is ever original and resourceful, is right), also presupposes a cosmic static background (over and above Chidakasha—ether of Consciousness), which is the Mahakundali Shakti in the Chinmayadeha (body of Consciousness) of Parameshvara or Parameshvari (the Supreme Lord in male an female aspect). In the earliest stage of creation, when the world arises only as a mist in Divine Consciousness, it requires, as the principle or pole of Tat (That), the correlate principle or pole of Aham (I); in the development of the former, the latter serves as the static background. In our own experiences, too, 'Apperception' or consciousness of self is the sustaining background—a string, so to say, which holds together all the loose beads of our elements of feeling. The sustaining ground or Adhara, as the seat of static force, therefore is found, in one form or other, in every phase and stage of creative evolution. The absolute or ultimate form is, of course, Chit-Shakti (Consciousness as power) itself, the unfailing light of awareness about which our Gayatri (Mantra) says: 'Which sustains and impels all the activities of Buddhi.' This fact is symbolised by the Kali-murti: not a mere symbol, however.

"2. My remarks about the rising or awakening of the Serpent Power at the Muladhara have been, perhaps, almost of the nature of a paradox. The coiled power, though awakened, uncoiled, and rising, never really stirs from its place; only a sort of 'ethereal double' or 'eject' is unloosed and sent up through the system of centers. Now, in plain language, this ethereal double or eject means the dynamic equivalent of the static power concentrated at the Mula, or root. Whenever by Pranayama of Bijamantra, or any other suitable means, the Muladhara becomes, like an electro-magnetic machine, oversaturated (though the Kundali

Shakti at the Mula is infinite and exhaustless, yet the capacity of a given finite organism to contain it in a static form is limited, and therefore there may be oversaturation), a dynamic or operative equivalent of the static power is set up, possibly by a law similar to Nature's law of induction, by which the static power itself is not depleted or rendered other than static. It is not that static energy at the Mula wholly passes over into a dynamic form – the coiled Kundali leaving the Mula, thus making it a void; that cannot be, and, were it so, all dynamic operation in the body would cease directly for want of a background. The coiled power remains coiled or static, and yet something apparently passes out of the Mula–viz., the dynamic equivalent. This paradox can perhaps be explained in two ways:

"(a) One explanation was suggested in my main letter. The potential Kundali Shakti becomes partly converted into kinetic Shakti, and yet, since Shakti, even as given in the Mula-center, is an infinitude, it is not depleted; the potential store always remains unexhausted. I referred to a passage in the Upanishad about Purna. In this case the dynamic equivalent is a partial conversion of one mode of energy into another. In Laya-Yoga (here described) it is ordinarily so. When, however, the infinite potential becomes an infinite kinetic—when, that is to say, the coiled power at the Mula becomes absolutely uncoiled—we have necessarily the dissolution of the three bodies (Sthula, Linga, and Karana—gross, subtle, and causal), and consequently Videhamukti (bodiless liberation), because the static background in relation to a particular form of existence has now wholly given way, according to our hypothesis. But Mahakundali remains; hence individual Mukti (liberation) need not mean dissolution of Samsara (transmigrating worlds) itself. Commonly, however, as the Tantra says, 'Pitva pitva punah pitva,' etc.[7]

"(b) The other explanation is suggested by the law of induction. Take an electromagnetic machine: [8]if a suitable substance be placed near it, will induce in it an equivalent and opposite kind of electro-magnetism [8]

7. "Having drunk, having drunk, having again drunk", a passage in the Kularnava Tantra signifying not actual drinking (as some suppose), but repeated raising of Kundalini.

8. We may say "Take a magnet" and "magnetism".

40

without loosing its own stock of energy.
In conduction, energy flows over into another thing, so that the source loses and
the other thing gains what it has lost,
and its gain is similar in kind to the loss.
Not so induction. There the source does
not lose, and the induced energy is equivalent
and opposite in kind to the inducing energy. Thus a positive charge will induce an
equivalent negative charge in a neighbouring
object. Now, shall we suppose that the
Muladhara, when it becomes over-saturated, induces in the neighbouring centre (say,
Svadhishthana) a dynamic (not static) equivalent? [9] Is this what the rise of the Serpent Power really means? The explanation,
I am tempted to think, is not perhaps altogether fantastic."

9.—Here is the seat of the first moving, or Pashyanti Shabda.

THE ASANS OF YOGA

The first Asan gives strength, and cures diseases of the muscles and nerves of the body. There are eighty-four Asans. Some of them are used to retain youth; others are used to produce calm, peace and harmony.

THE PRATYAHARE YOGA

This Yoga is the best for controlling lust, passions, etc. It is used to stop the thinking principle, or bring the mind under control. The lower mind is ignorance itself, and until this fluttering mind is made to come to one point, the blessed state of peace cannot be attained.

All danger is caused by ignorance. There is no danger that comes from wisdom.

"He is mightier who controls his spirit, than he who conquers the city."

All the dangers come from uncontrolled mind. If every one would control the mind, all the miseries of this world would cease. All inharmony in the home is caused by lack of understanding of each other, and uncontrolled thoughts.

When people learn to control themselves and understand each other, then the poor Judge of the divorce courts will be relieved.

42

MUDRAS MOVE THE KUNDALINI

There are Eighty-four Mudras in Yoga.

Why do Yogins practice Mudras and the five Dharanas?

To control the five Life or Vital Forces that are working in the human body. When these five forces are controlled, Yogins attain emancipation, or liberation.

What are the five forces and from whence they come?

The names of these forces are: Prana, Apana, Samana, Vyana, and Udana, and they come from the Kundalini. They are part of the Kundalini's energy (dynamic).

Through Mudras the Yogins succeed in gathering these five forces together, bringing them to their home, the Mother Kundalini, which is sleeping at the Muladhara Chakra, as Static energy of the Mother of the Universe. Yogins force the Prana and Apana to the place where this Static energy of the Kundalini is sleeping. Thus they awaken her.

First. The Earth Dharana. "When the Yogin opens the 'Earth Chakra' by the power of the Kundalini, he conquers the earth,

43

and no earthly element can injure him. He walks over the land, freed from death."

Second. The Water Dharana. "Next the Yogin moves the Kundalini energy up to the second Chakra—the 'Water Chakra'. By opening this Chakra the Yogin is free from all sorrow, no water can ever harm him. Although he be thrown in the deepest water, "he will never die in the water." This Mudra should be kept very carefully secret, as by revealing this, success is lost."

Third, The Fire Dharana. "The Yogin should move the Kundalini energy up to the 'Fire Chakra.' When the Yogin opens this Chakra, known as Fire Dharana—the killer of the fear of death—then "fire can not harm or burn the Yogin." What else is there for him to fear?"

Fourth, The Air Dharana. "The Yogin opens this Chakra by bringing the Kundalini energy upward, and as soon as he has succeeded in opening the 'Air Chakra,' he has mastered levitation. This Mudra is the destroyer of death, and the Yogin will never be disturbed by air. This can not be taught to the faithless; by doing so all success would be lost."

44

Fifth,. The Ether Dharana. "Here the Yogin moves the energy of the Mother Kundalini upward and opens the 'Ether Chakra.' As soon as he is successful in opening this Chakra, he has opened the door of liberation or emancipation— he will never die unless he wills it."

"When the Yogin has learned the five Dharanas, the human body can visit and re-visit the Heavens, and he can go wherever he likes, as swiftly as the mind.

"Yogins should also practice the Bhastrika Kumbhaka. That, too, will awaken the Kundalini. He should move or awaken the Kundalini again and again, and though he be in the mouth of death, he need not fear it.

"When the Apana rises upward to the 'Fire Chakra,' the flame of divine fire grows strong and bright, being fanned by Apana. When the Apana fire mixes with the Prana, which is naturally hot, the spiritual heat of the body becomes bright and powerful." When the Kundalini feels this extra heat, she will awaken from sleep; then she goes into the Sushumna. As a key can open a door, so Yogi should open the door of liberation by awakening the Kundalini. The

Kundalini is coiled like a serpent, and by Mudra or Pranayama processes the Kundalini will certainly move and open the mouth of the Sushumna.

"Without moving the Kundalini, there are no other means that will clear away the impurities of the 7200 Nadis.

"Yogins should practice the Bhastrika Ku mbhaka, three hours daily; then he need have no fear of death.

"The Great Goddess Kundalini, the Energy of the Self, sleeps in the Muladhara. She has the form of a serpent, having three coils and a half. As long as she is asleep in the body, (finer body), the jiva is a mere animal, and true wisdom does not arise, though Yogi may practice ten million Yoga.

"When Kundalini is sleeping it is awakened by the kind Guru (the spiritual teacher); then all the Chakra's knots are pierced, and the Prana then goes thru the Sushumna. The mind is then controlled, and the Yogi arises above death. Yogi should practice daily some of the following Mudras: Maha Mudra, Nabho Mudra, Udiyana, Maha Bandha, Maha Vedha, Kechari, Jalandhara, Yoni, Viparitakarna, Kaki, Sambhavi and others.

"Maha Mudra should be practiced with the Jalanhara Bandha. Practice of this Mudra will cure fever, bowel trouble, enlargement of the spleen, indigestion, consumption, leprosy and any other diseases. It will awaken the Kundalini. It is called the Great Mudra by the wise. Practice of the Mudras should be equal on both sides.

"The Nabho Mudra should be practiced, and it is easy to practice. It, too, makes the Yogi safe from all diseases, and the body never becomes old but keeps perpetual youth.

"The Maha Bandha Mudra should be practiced with Jalandhara Mudra, which will bring the Prana downward. He who practices this Mudra will control the Prana and Aprana and move the Kundalini.

"The Maha Vedha Mudra is the best Mudra to awaken the Kundalini, b u t should be practiced with the Bandha and Maha Bandha. It gives success to Yogi over all nature's finer forces.

"Yogi should practice in secret, and not tell any one if he desires success.

The Udiyana, or Flying Up Mudra, moves the Goddess Kundalini, and who masters this Mudra will be Master of all

powers, like levitation, etc. This Mudra
makes it easy to attain emancipation, and is
the key that unlocks the door of liberation.

"The Mula Bandha Mudra is the best
Mudra to control the Apana and Prana,
and is the key to everlasting youth. Mix-
ing the Prana and Apana causes heat in the
body; that heat causes the Kundalini to awak
en—then she goes upward thru the Sushumna. In that Sushumna all wisdom and powers are.

"Jalandhara Mudra is the well tried
Mudra for keeping old age, decay and
death away. It saves the nectar and keeps
the vital force moving in the right Nadi.
Who practices this Mudra daily, becomes
an adept. Yogi should practice Maha Bandha, Udiyana and Jalandhara all at once.

"Khechari Mudra is the King of all the
'Mudras. It is hard to attain. The Yogi who
masters it even for half an hour, will overcome hunger, thirst, decay and death—his
body becomes divine. The earth, water, fire,
air and ether can not harm that body. Yoni
Mudra, Viparitakaran Mudra, Vajroni
Mudra, Sakti Mudra, Manduki Mudra and
Sambhavi Mudra are well tried, and will
awaken the Kundalini.

48

"The five Dharanas should be learned from a Master. With these Dharanas a Yogi goes wherever he wants to with his physical body; he may go to Heaven, walk on water, air and fire and is Master of All. Except for the practice of Kundalini, what other means are there to purify the Nadis? Once setting this power moving, Yogi should practice constantly. Who can practice a yama, need have no fear of death. Hatha Yoga and Raja Yoga should be practiced together, as Hatha Yoga is dependent upon Raja Yoga and Raja Yoga is dependent upon Hatha Yoga. These Mudras should not be taught to the wicked and faithless, but they should be taught to calm, peaceful and faithful students. And he who teaches the secret of the Mudras is the real Guru. He can be called Ishwar (God), in human form.

"What more shall tell, O Devi? There is nothing in this world like the Mudras to attain the human goal quickly and successfully."

THE POWER OF THE PRANAYAMA YOGA.

What is Pranayama? It is the stepping stone of the Yogi, or in other words the foundation, the helpmate of the Yogi in controlling his enemies—freeing him from diseases. The Pranayama is the means by which the Yogi masters levitation, walks upon the water, and also the means of living buried alive for years. Pranayama is the Master Key by which Yogis open the door of liberation, and master all the forces.

Pranayama is the best method for suffering humanity to overcome diseases, conquer fear, overcome nervousness or despondency. It opens the door of Blessed Peace, it gives hope to the hopeless, power to the poor, faith to the faithless. There is no other way to control the mind, as mind is nothing without desire or thought; desires and thoughts are nothing without Prana.

What is Prana? Prana is everything.

"Prana is Fire; Prana is the Sun; the Cloud; the Wind; Prana is the Killer of Demons; Prana is the Earth. It is what is and is not, immortal. * * * Prana is the center of everything."–Prasna Upanishad.

Prana is like the forces of electricity. Everything that moves is moved by Prana. Prana moves the lungs, then air goes in and out as breath. Prana is back of everything as force. The mind is lord of the senses and the organs–the Prana is lord of the mind: The mind is the motor–the Prana is the power that moves the motor.

The Prana is the great power of the Mother Kundalini. From the Prana there are born other Pranas, namely,–Apana, Samana, Vyana, and Udana. These are in the various parts of the body, but Prana is the power back of All and All.

How do Yogis control this power? By Pranayama. Prana is the Vital or life force –Yama, how to control it. This is why Yogis call Pranayama the stepping stone, or helpmate.

Let us see what H. Y. Pradipika, the most famous, says: "When the breath is irregular, the mind wanders, but when the breath is under control the mind is also under control. Because of this, Yogis live as long as they want to."

Everyone should learn to control the breath, by the practice of Pranayama. "Man lives as long as he has breath in his body. When the breath goes out he is said to be dead."

"As long as the Nadis (nerves) are not pure, the Prana can not go through the Sushumna, and as long as Prana does not go through the Sushumna there is no success for the Yogi. As soon as the Nadis are purified, the Yogi succeeds in doing Pranayama, and then his body becomes slender and light. This is the sign of Pranayama success, for then the Prana goes through the Sushumna.

"There is no success without purification of the Nadis, and there is no purification of the Nadis without Pranayama.

"The Brahma (God of Creation), devotes himself to the practice of Pranayama, and is free from the fear of death.

"When Prana goes through the Sushumna, the mind becomes one-pointed. This is called Unmani Avastha (the steadiness of the mind).

"It is through the practice of Pranayama Yoga, that Yogi attains Sidhis (master over

Nature's Forces, Levitation, etc.).

"By forcing the Prana downward and raising the Apana upward, the Yogi becomes young, though he be old in years."

There are eight different Pranayamas, that should be learned from a teacher who has mastered them. Any of the Pranayama practice can cure the diseases of the nervous system, as countless testimonial letters on file will show, as Rev. A. K. Burkland, Miss E. Lindsay and others.

The same authority says further: "When Pranayama, called Kevala Kumbhaka, has been mastered, there is nothing in the three worlds that can not be attained."

It is by the power of Pranayama that the Yogis do the wonderful feats of levitation, walking on water, etc. This is not their goal —they only want liberation—but there is no liberation without awakening the Kundalini.

If the busy people of the world will practice Pranayama just a few months, they will be happily surprised to see its effect upon the body and mind. The body will become light and active. Idleness will vanish like darkness before the light.

Pranayama is easy to practice. Any one

can do it, the young, the old, diseased or maimed. It is the key to everlasting youth.

"Pranayama will have a wonderfully soothing effect on one whenever they are at war with themselves. They will gain instantaneous peace. Is the world going hard with you? Do you feel you are losing out in the race of life? Then I say, practice Pranayama; after the practice you will emerge wonderfully renewed and renascent, ready to forge ahead in the battle of life, with new vigour, new faith in yourself and new hope. Are you face to face with a problem that requires a cool brain and clear thinking, profound and mature judgement? My advice to you is that before tackling the problem, attain mental poise by practicing Pranayama. There is nothing like it for giving poise, peace and balance. In the midst of the greatest stress and storm, in the thick of the battle, steady yourself for a supreme effort by practicing Pranayama. Practice this daily without fail, and you will notice how marvellously, your mental, physical and spiritual powers, are developed. You will then always be master of yourself and of the situation. You will always have a tremendous amount of surplus energy, mentally, physically and spiritually, upon which to draw.

"This will make your life natural and peaceful, free from nervous exhaustion and worry, because it will enable you to keep your vital force of life ever renewed and reenforced. It will enable you to charge your battery, to electrify it every day. To-day you resemble a small boat tossing on the waves of a stormy life without oars, at the mercy of wind and wave, always in danger of rocks and shoals. Practice Pranayama and you will plough thru the vast sea of life like a giant dreadnought.

"Learn Pranayama—practice Pranayama, and be master of yourself and your circumstances." Excerpt from the Author's Pranayama - Lessons Three and Four.

THE POWER OF DHARANA, DHIYA-NA, AND SAMYAMA YOGA.

The different practices of Dharana Yoga to control the mind power and attain success are stepping stones in Yoga.

Thru the power of Dharana Yoga, Yogis have proven that they can control every function of the body, such as heart action etc.; also controlling wild beasts, reptiles, etc..

Sending thought directions to one when he looses his way. I have been helped many times by my Master thru the power of Dharana Yoga, as once being lost in the mountains ,and again when there was no food or shelter, he sent me telepathic messages directing me which way I should go, although he was hundreds of miles from the place where I was. The power of Dharana is the most wonderful of the wonderous.

Once when sitting by the Master in a small town, a chicken-hawk swooped down upon a small chicken. The little fellow fought for his life. The mother hen did all she could by fighting and squalling, but that was not enough, the poor chicken was in the mouth of death. The Master looked up at the hawk once and the hawk and chicken came to earth. Then and there both were friendly, and remained in the company of each other for some time. It was a great joy for me to see a chicken and a hawk associating together peacefully—it was indeed heavenly.

At sunset my Master once again looked upon the chicken and the hawk; lo, at once the chicken ran to his mother, and the hawk flew in the air. That was all done by the power of Samyama.

What is Samyama and Dharana? It is of three kinds: gross, subtle and luminous. Mastery of mind and developement of will. What is will? Yogis know will is power. It can do anything for you and will set you free. The Master said: "By will man may become a Deva (like God), or the opposite." The Bible says: "As a man thinketh in his heart, so is he." The difference between a human being and the Divine: man desires the God will, His will works. As long as man desires, yet doubts his power, the doubt is the killer.

Make up your mind. Stick with the will, that you **can** do a thing, and it is then already half done. But when you doubt in yourself—that you **can not**, it will never be done. You develop the will and become like Brahma.

The Yogis open the inner eye by Dharana, and by opening the inner eye nature becomes like an open book. There is nothing hidden from them. They see their inner body as an ordinary man sees the outer body. They see how the different glands work; see the connection between the two bodies, the gross and the subtle; see where the Chakras are, see, the five Pranas and know how to gather them together to hold on one Chakra to open it. They know all.

Why do we not all see such things as the Yogis see? Because the Yogis have developed their inner eye and have made their mind a great faculty.

This can be compared to the great telescope. As the great telescope reveals the hidden secrets of the stars, so the inner eye of the Yogi reveals to him what he was, what is

God and where He is. Yogi found That (God) within himself.

Nothing is hidden from God; so nothing from Yogi. The scientists and others may call the Yogi whatever they wish, as very often Yogis are called fakes, etc. The blame is not with the scientists or scoffers, but is due to their ignorance, as they are ignorant of the blessed powers of the Yogi or the power that is hidden within every one.

The following excerpt from the "San Antonio Light", of March 2, 1930.—"American Magazine Section." This is a remarkable full page article, with complete illustrations.

"The distinguished New York nerve specialist, Dr. Frederick Tilney, declared in his recent book on the development of the human brain that this organ is still used to only a small percentage of its real capacity. Dr. Constantin von Economo, of Vienna, as distinguished in European neurology as is Dr. Tilney in the United States, has stated this belief even more definitely.

"Both these experts had chiefly in mind, their statements make clear, the intelligence of the human mind and its power to make correct judgments. They might have said virtually the same things, however, about the power of the will to control both mind and body.

"For generations these powers of the will have been well known in special instances, like the fakirs of India or the religious fanatics who lie on beds of sharp spikes, who beat themselves in frenzy and yet feel no pain. Now scientific men are coming to the opinion that all human minds possess much these same powers of developed will. All that is necessary is that the latent power of the mind be appreciated and applied.

In a recent hospital case the patient, not wishing to take an anesthetic, merely went to sleep by will power, first telling the surgeon to go ahead. Other patients examined scientifically by the doctors turn out to have the ability of stopping the heart beat temporarily or of interrupting the normal pulse in the wrist, all by the power of the will. Sight, hearing, smell and other senses may be either decreased or increased in sensitivity by will power. Determination, long supposed to be a useful virtue only in some kind of contest, turns out to be as valuable in man's contest with his own body as anywhere else.

"The Indian fakirs, long supposed by many people to be merely cheats and liars, but now recognized by scientific men as possessing unusual powers of mental control of the body, are still perhaps the best examples of what the will can do to bodily machinery. Not long ago one of these fakirs, Tahra Bey, gave in London an exhibition to which numerous medical men were invited. Forty physicians and scientists sat on the stage of the theatre where the exhibition was given. All were permitted to examine the fakir during the demonstrations. Trickery was virtually impossible and experts agree that none was used.

"Some of Tahra Bey's demonstrations were familiar ones of stage hypnotists. Throwing himself into a trance-like state, he made his body quite rigid. The stiff body was then laid on a series of sabres, not fully sharp but still edged enough to be uncomfortable. A large stone was laid on the fakir's rigid chest and was pounded with a sledge.

"Brought out of his rigid condition, the fakir then thrust hat pins through his cheeks, and through folds of flesh on chest and arms. A penknife similarly thrust through a fold of flesh produced a bleeding wound, or a bloodless one, whichever the fakir suggested and announced in advance. Like his predecessors in India, Tahra Bey then lay down on a bed of six-inch nails driven point upward through a wooden door and reclined on this remarkable couch while an assistant weighing about 160 pounds stood for several minutes on the fakir's chest.

"After this demostration the fakir's back, examined by some of the physicians present, showed distinct marks of the points of the nails but no blood was shed and the fakir claimed to feel no pain. That the hat points and knives were actually thrust through the flesh and that some of these wounds actually did not bleed as they would have done in normal bodies, was also attested by the medical committee.

"No claim was made by this particular fakir of anything supernatural in his performance, nor is any such claim in the least justified. That anyone can accomplish very much the same feats with

60

some training and a strong enough will is proved by the fact that many persons have done so; notably a Parisian sceptic named Paul Heuze, who disbelieved the supernatural claims of some of the earlier fakirs and managed, it is said, with but one rehearsal, to duplicate the feats of lying on the bed of nails and of thrusting pins and knives into his flesh without causing pain or drawing blood.

"Last year there was prominent in Berlin a still more remarkable example of this kind of bodily control by will power; a miner named Paul Diebel who similarly was able to thrust knives into his body, to cut himself without bleeding and even to allow arrows to be shot into his chest without apparent harm. One of Diebel's tricks which attracted great attention was an apparent ability to bleed at will from his skin, as well as to prevent bleeding.

"One theory held by physiologists is that the living cells which make up the nerves and which ordinarily are in contact with each other so that nerve messages can pass, withdraw a little at their points of contact so that the nerve path is broken. The diagrams of the Hindu fakir on this page illustrate the process. Apparently an effort of the will sometimes can accomplish this breaking of the nerve circuits, much as can be done by drugs like cocaine, which are used as anesthetics. In both instances the nerve break means, that no messages of pain or other sensations can pass to the brain. Control of the will over the flow of blood is equally well established by scientific evidence. Dr. A. S. Hyman, of New York City, has published accounts of three patients who were able by efforts of their will completely to stop the pulse in the wrist; the pulse which a physician usually feels when he wishes to count the rate of the heartbeat. An East Indian physician, Dr. Vasant G. Rele, has described similarly and at length the characteristics of an Indian holy man whose abilities in similar directions were examined by a committee of physicians in Bombay.

"This Yogi was able, the physicians found, to stop the pulse beat in either arm for more than two minutes. The pulse in his temple on either side could be stopped similarly. Even the heart of this man stopped beating for six seconds by the physician's watch, when ordered to do so by the owner's will.

"What happens in the case of the Yogis, fakirs and others who can control bleeding or pulse beats is, the scientists believe, that these nerves, not ordinarily subject to control by the mind, are trained by long practice and efforts of the will to respond to voluntary orders.

Much the same thing happens when people train the muscles of their scalps to obey orders from nerves now feeble and unused, so that these people can move their ears a little as man's animal ancestors used to do

"Even life and death may be affected by the will. Major H. E. Smith, Assistant Police Commissioner of the Gold Coast Colony, in Africa, recently reported an instance in which a highly intelligent native willed himself to die as a result of a quarrel and supposed witchcraft. Even on his body atter death Europan physicians could discover no reason whatsover for death or even for illness.

"But if a strong will can stop a fakir's heartbeat at will, make him bleed or not bleed at will, certainly it can keep anybody from yielding to weakness or crime."

How do Yogis develop that power? I am sorry this cannot be explained in a book. It can only be taught to those who are seeking truth, not to the faithless. But I will explain as much as can be given in any book.

First I will give the idea of Samyama from Katha Upanished: "The Wise should sink the Speech into Mind. Mind should sink into Intellect. Intellect should sink into Self. The Self should sink into the Great Self. The Great Self should sink into Eternal Peace (Self-God).

First. Lips should close, ears should open.

Second. Mind should stop wandering about.

Third. Thoughts should be suppressed, the Intuition should be developed.

Fourth. Intuition should be suppressed

and Ego should be felt.

Fifth. Ego should be merged, blended into the Great Self.

The Great Self into Self Peace." (God—Universal Soul).

The above reference is to the practice of Yoga known as Samyama.

What the Yogi gains by Samyama. "The direct perception gives the Yogi the right meaning, the inspiration gives him the word, the intuition gives him the right conclusion and discrimination saves him from error." The Yogi sees the truth face to face.

Any one can develop the above power by daily practice of Yoga. "But man can become aware of things which the senses can't grasp, Budhigrahyam atiudriyam (the reason or intellect) The proof of this you can get daily, when the Yogi's power is developed. This fact that man can see with his Budhi (intellect), the truth about a thing he has never seen or known before, is enough to destroy the materialistic idea of thought.

"What is knowledge? In what does it consist? We must distinguish between knowledge in itself and the means of knowledge. Again, among the means we must distinguish between the instruments and the operations performed with the instruments.

"By Knowledge we means awareness, taking a thing into active consciousness, into our Chaitanyam. But when we say, taking it into our Chaitanyam. what do we imply? Whence do we take it? The European says from outside, we say from inside, from Chaitanyam itself. In other words, all knowledge is an act of consiousness operating on something in the consciousness itself. In the first place everything we know exists in Parabrahma, that is, in our indivisible, universal self-existence. It is there, but not yet expressed, not vyakta. Then it exists in pure Chit (the essential consciousness of the Spirit), which is the womb of things as an idea of form, name and quality. It has name, form and quality in the Karana or Mahat, the casual, typal and ideal state of consciousness. Then it gets the possibility of change, development or modification in the Sukshma, the subtle, mental or plastic state of consciousness. Finally it gets the actual change, development, modification or evolution in the Sthula, the material or evolutionary state of consciousness. In the Karana there is no evolution, nothing ever changes, all is eternal.

64

The Karana is Satyam. In the Sukshma all
is preparation of change; it is full of imagination or anritam, therefore it is Swap-
pa, not really false, but not immediate-
ly applicable to the Karana or Sthu-
la. In the Sthula all evolves. It is partial satyam developing by the turning of old Satyam developing by the turning of old sat-
tion, and the turning of new anritam into
new satyam, which is called creation. In the
satyam, which is called creation. In the
Karana there is no creation, no birth, no
death, all exists for ever—the only change is
from type to type, from fulfilment to fulfilment.

"Therefore to know is really to
be conscious of the thing in any or
all of these three states. The knowledge of the Sthula is science. The knowledge of the Sukshma is philosophy, religion and metaphysics. The knowledge of
the Karana is Yoga. When a man knows the
Sthula, he knows it with his senses, that is,
with the Manas, he knows the Sukshma with
reason of the inspired intellect, he knows the
Karana with the Jnanam or spiritual realization. Therefore complete knowledge
consists of three operations, first, objec-

tive Upalabdhi or experience, secondly, intellectual statement of your understanding of the thing, thirdly, subjective Upalabdhi or spiriual experience. The scientist begins from the bottom and climbs if he can, to the top. The Yogin begins from the top and descends for perfect proof to the bottom. You are not scientists, you are sadhaks. Therefore, when you speak of knowledge you must understand the process; you realise a thing by subjective experience, Bhava, then, think about it and formulate your experience in Artha and Vak, the combination which forms thought; you verify or test your experience by physical or objective experience.

"For instance you see a man. You want to know what he is, what he thinks and what he does. How does the scientist or the material man do it? He watches the man, he notes what he says, what are his expressions of speech and face, what are his actions, what sort of people he lives with, etc. All this is objective. Then he reasons from his objective experience. He says— "The man says this or that, so he must think so and so or he must have such and such a character; his actions show the same," his face shows the same, and so he goes on reasoning. If

he dies not gets all the necessary facts,
he fills them up from his imagination of from his memory, that is his
experience of other men, of himself or of
human life as read of in books or heard of
from other people. He perceives, he observes,
contrasts, compares, deducts, infers, ima-
gines, remembers and the composite result he
calls reason, knowledge, fact. In reality he
has arrived at a probability, for it is impossible for him to be sure that his conclusions
are correct or anything indeed correct in his
thought, except the actual observation, perceptions of his eye, ear, nose, touch and taste.
Anything beyond this the material man dis-
trusts. Nothing is true to him except what he
observes with his senses or what agrees with
his sensory perceptions.

"Now what does the Yogin do? He simply puts himself into relation with the thing
itself. Not with its form, name or quality but
with itself. He may never have seen the form,
heard the name or had experience of the quality, but still he can know the thing. Because
it is the thing itself and it is in himself and
one with himself, that is in the Mahakarana
in a man. There all meet the Atman and are
so entirely one with the Atman that by mere-

ly being in contact with it, I can know everything about it. Few Yogins reach that state. But all the same, even in the Karana I can put myself in relation with the thing and know it by Bhava. I put myself, my soul, into relation with the soul of the man I study or the thing I study; Prajna in me becomes one with the Prajna in him or it. How do I do this? Simply by becoming passive and facing him or it in my Buddhi. If my Buddhi is quite pure or fairly purified, if my Manas is shanta, then I get the truth about him. I get it by Bhava, by spiritual or subjective realization.

"Then I have to make the thing I have got clear and precise. To do that I must state it intellectually to my mind, that is, I must think about it. I have these ideas I am telling you in myself as unexpressed knowledge; they shape themselves in words, Vak, and take on a precise meaning, Artha. That is thought. Most people think vaguely; half expressing the thing in an imperfect Vak and a partial Artha. The Yogin must not do that. His thoughts must express themselves in clear and perfect sentences. He may know a thing without thinking it out, but if he thinks, he must think clearly and perfectly.

"The Yogin reasons when necessary, but not like the man of science. He sees the thing with his prophetic power interpreting the truth into thought; the pratyaksha gives him the Artha, the inspiration gives him the Vak, the intuition gives him the right conclusion about it, the right siddhanta, the Viveka guards him from error. Behold the truth by these four simple operations perfectly thought out. If he has to argue, then the intuition gives him the right arguments. He has not to proceed painfully from one syllogism to another as the logician does.

"Finally, he verifies his knowledge by the facts of the objective world. He has seen the truth about the man by merely looking at him or at the idea of him; he has thought it out clearly and now he compares his idea with the man's action, speech etc. Not to test his truth; for he knows that a man's action, speech etc. only partially express the man and mislead the student; but in order to see how the truth he knows from the Karana is being worked out in the Sthula. He trusts the man's objective life only so far as it is in agreement with the deeper truth he has gained by Yoga.

"You see the immense difference. The

only difficulty is that you have been accustomed to use the senses and the reason to the subordination and almost to the exclusion of the higher faculties. Therefore you find it difficult to make the higher faculties active.

"If only you could start from the beginning, with the Bhava, the Atmajnana, how easy it would be! That will yet happen. But first, you have to get rid of the lower Buddhi, of the Indriyas in the manas, and awaken the activity of the higher faculties. They will see for you, hear for you, as well as think for you.

First, then, get your sankaras right. Understand intellectually what I have told you and will yet tell you. Then by use of the Will, keep the reason, imagination, memory, thought, sensations sufficiently quiet for the higher Buddhi to know itself as separate and different from these lower qualities. As the higher separates itself and becomes more and more active, the lower, already discouraged, will become less and less active and finally trouble you no more.

Therefore Will first, then by Will, by Shakti, the Jnanam. First Kali, then Surya.

I shall explain the various faculties when I have finished with the rest of the system."

From "Yogic Sadhan"

By Master Arabinda Ghose.

SAMADHI YOGA

"Salutation to the Siva, who is in the form of power of all science, the Nada and Bindu. Any one devoted to these will obtain the state which is above the Maya,"

Samadhi is many stages, but any Samadhi can destroy the enemy death, and bring one to the Divine State of Supreme Bliss.

When the Prana (Vital or Life Force) and mind are controlled, a state of harmony arises—that is Samadhi. As salt thrown in water becomes one with the water, so the controlled mind becomes one with Atma—that is Samadhi.

"Those who really understand the greatness of Yoga, and obtain it thru practice, and by the help of a kind Guru, are emancipated.

"Understanding of Wisdom, and directly realizing the one Atma as Parabrahma (Universal Soul) is emancipation, and it gives power over all of Nature's forces—known as Sidhis and Anima."

"Without the help of a Spiritual teacher, and without sincere effort of the student, the real realization of Truth, and the state of

Samadhi cannot be attained by the student."

"When a Yogi has awakened the Kundalini (Mother God) by practicing the Mudras, then Prana moves thru the Sushumna, and having aroused all the Chakras, the Yogi arises above all Karma, and is then freed from cause and effect;—that state is Samadhi.

"The mind is the cause of Karma; when the mind and Prana (its moving power) is controlled by daily practice of Mudras, then the lower mental activity ceases. The higher self then manifests. Yogi attains the unchanging state. He is master over time, matter and space;—that state is Samadhi. When the mind is poised, the Prana moves in the Sushumna, and real realization is obtained. Why should one fear death, as they are above decay and death? No one can attain wisdom as long as the Prana and mind are not controlled. He who controls the Prana and mind attain liberation.

"Many say liberation can be only attained by Wisdom; then what is the use of Yoga?" The Siva answered: "A battle is won by a sword; but what is the use of a sword without a warrior and valor? So both are needed." "Those great men and women have attained pure wisdom and liberation

73

have not practiced Yoga, have they?" "They
have practiced Yoga in their past lives."

I will drop this matter here as I do not
want to prove or spend any time on the
past. My object is to show how to awaken
the Kundalini and reach the blessed state of
Samadhi.

The human body has a great number of
Nadis, the three main ones,—Ida and Pingala on each side of the spine, the Sushumna in the middle. The Prana moves thru
the Ida and Pingala only; the Sushumna
being closed. When Yogi learns the secret
of controlling the Prana and Apana, then
he can awaken the Kundalini, and force the
Prana to go thru the Sushumna. When this
has been accomplished—Samadhi follows.
All other means are waste of time. Thus Yogi should not follow other means if he desires
to awaken the Kundalini and reach Samadhi.

The mind is made to move by two things,
the Prana and desire. If Prana is controlled,
desire is also controlled. Therefore, the Prana and mind are as one. As long as the mind
is not mastered, so long the senses are not
mastered. When the three are controlled,
then the Yoga can hold them on any Chakra,
and awaken or move the Kundalini. By

control of the Prana and mind the Yogi gains strength; by this strength he arises above all diseases. So Yogi should practice Pranayama and the Mudras to master Prana.

The mind is the master of the organs of sense, the Prana is the master of the mind. When the Prana and the mind are under control the Yogi attains blessed peace, which can only be known by experience.

The lower mind is ignorance itself. When the mind is controlled, ignorance, which is the Mother of Maya (illusion), dies. The Yogi attains Samadhi or the state of Brahma.

Every one wishes to attain the Laya Yoga, but it is difficult to attain. To do so the Shambhavi Mudra is the best to practice. This Mudra cannot be attained until the Prana and the mind are controlled; then Shambhavi Mudra should be practiced as it raises the Yogi above time, matter, space and ether. He controls the power of nature's forces, as levitation and walking on water, and he can live as long as he desires. but this is not the object of the Hindu Yogis. Their object is not to attain wonderful powers. but Seedless Samadhi—the Brahmic state—which is above all other states; it is divine peace and common to all.

When the Yogi succeeds in controlling Prana, from the Ida and Pingala Nadis, and makes it go thru the Sushumna, he has reached the state wherein he experiences TRUTH, which is the Light of Lights, and is the Source of All. This is the goal of all.

Yogis practice different Mudras to control Prana. When Prana is controlled and made to move thru the Sushumna, the state of Samadhi follows. This is the correct method When Yogi desires to cheat death and time, he raises the Prana up to the Ajna Chakra, placing the Prana and the mind in the Kudalini, then by steady meditation Yogi moves the Kundalini. He then places the Atma in the Brahma and Brahma in the Atama. He is then in Samadhi—ALL in ALL.

The external worlds are created by the lower mind. By controlling the lower mind, the external world is finished. Then meditating on the One Reality, the Yogi becomes that Reality or Brahma. He is not affected by matter, space or time. He is above all.

All things in the world are perceived by mind. When the mind is controlled there remains no duality. When the mind is merged

76

in the Atma, that state is the Absolute, and is Satchitanada (truth, wisdom, bliss).

"Salutation to Sushumna, to the Kundalini, to the Stream of Nectar flowing from the Moon".

The Nada Practice:

The Great Yogin Garakhnath has given out the practice of Nada to help those who are unable to realize the pure truth.

The Yogi should sit in the Sidhasan and practice the Shambhavi Mudra, and should listen with fixed mind to the sound of the self, which will be heard in the right side of the head. The sounds will be ten—from the ocean roar to a very subtle sound—but Yogi should keep the mind fixed on Nada which is the goal. When the Yogi is sitting in Sidhasan practicing Shambhavi with Yoni Mudra, he should force the Prana to the heart center, as the sound begins there. When Prana becomes one with the Nada, then the Yogi should move it to the Vishudha Chakra. As soon as Yogi succeeds in taking the Nada with Prana to the Vishudha Chakra, he will become like Devas, and the Brahmanada (Divine Bliss) will surely follow.

From the Vishudha Chakra Yogi should forcibly take the Prana and the Nada to the Ajna Chakra. This is the source of all Sidhis. Reaching here the Yogi controls all the finer forces of nature and mental knowledge. He arises above nature's elements and mind, and is one with Atma, above the world's miseries. His mind is listening to the inner sound of the Nada,—it is the blessed joy that can be known by one who has attained that state.

One state more remains for the Yogi; that is going up from the Ajna Chakra to the Sir Chakra or the Thousand Petal Lotus. In Yogi will hear the sound of flutes. He has this Lotus, Yogi will hear the sound of flutes. He has then reached the highest state of Bliss. He is equal to God, as he can create and destroy any material thing, if he so wishes. But creation and destruction are not the object of the Yogi; he wants to be liberated, and in this State he is liberation itself.

"Practice of Nada is most easy, even a feeble minded person can succeed by daily practice. The practitioner will soon start to feel the joy that arises by the Nada in the heart. That joy cannot be explained by words as it is Divine Joy, above the reach of mental knowledge.

Sick and suffering humanity should practice Shambhavi, that they could hear the Nada sound, or the Inner Voice.

"Benefits to the students that practice Nada—as soon as their mind forms the habits of listening to the inner sound of the Nada, it will never be disturbed by external sounds. By daily practice of Nada, the mind becomes firm and attracted by Nada,—it surely becomes one with Nada. As the sharp goad is best to control the mad elephant, so the Nada is best to control the mind. The Nada holds the mind fixed, as a bird cannot fly without wings. Those Yogis who have mastered the Nada practice are never disturbed by any other sound; they are liberated and emancipated." —H. Y. Pradpika.

Yogi in Samadhi does not feel pain, thirst, hunger, heat or cold, nothing can harm him, his body does not decay, death never comes, near him. He is equal to God.

The Following is taken from The Yoga Aphorisms. - Chapter III – IV.

Translation and Commentary by

SWAMI VIVEKANANDA

1. Dharana is holding the mind on to some particular object.

2—An unbroken flow of knowledge in that object is Dhyana.

3—When that, giving up all forms, reflects only the meaning, it is Samadhi.

4—(These) three (when practiced) in regard to one object is Samyama.

5—By the conquest of that comes light of knowledge.

When one has succeeded in making this Samyama, all powers come under his control. This is the great instrument of the Yogi. The objects of knowledge are infinite, and they are divided into the gross, grosser, grossest, and the fine, finer, finest, and so on. This Samyama should be first applied to gross things, and when you begin to get knowledge of this gross, slowly, by stages, it should be brought to finer things.

6—That should be employed in stages.

This is a note of warning not to attempt to go too fast.

15—The succession of changes is the cause of manifold evolution.

16—By making Samyama on the three sorts of changes comes the knowledge of past and future.

We must not lose sight of the first definition of Samyama. When the mind has attained to that state when it identifies itself with the internal impression of the object, leaving the external, and when, by long practice, that is retained by the mind, and the mind can get into that state in a moment, that is Samyama. If a man in that state wants to know the past and future he has to make a Samyama on the changes in the Samskaras (111. 13). Some are working now at present, some have worked out, and some are waiting to work; so by marking a Samyama on these he knows the past and future.

21—By making Samyama on the form of the body, the perceptibility of the form being obstructed, and the power of manifestation in the eye being separated, the Yogi's body becomes unseen.

A Yogi standing in the midst of this room can apparently vanish. He does not really vanish, but he will not be seen by any one. The form and the body are, as it were, separated. You must remember that this can only be done when the Yogi has attained to that power of concentration when form and the thing formed have been separated. Then he makes a Samyama on that, and the power to perceive forms is obstructed, because the power of perceiving forms comes from the junction of form and the thing formed.

25—By making Samyama on the strength of the elephant, and others, their respective strength comes to the Yogi.

When a Yogi has attained to this Samyama and wants strength, he makes a Samyama on the strength of the elephant, and gets it. Infinite energy is at the disposal of every one, if he only knows how to get it. The Yogi has discovered the science of getting it.

26—By making Samyama on the effulgent light, (1.36) comes the knowledge of the fine, the obstructed and the remote.

When the Yogi makes Samyama on that effulgent light in the heart he sees things, which are very remote, things for instance, that are happening in a distant place, and which are obstructed by mountain barriers, and also things which are very fine.

39—When the cause of bondage of the Chitta has become loosened, the Yogi, by his knowledge of its channels of activity (the nerves), enters another's body.

The Yogi can enter a dead body, and make it get up and move, even while he himself is working in another body. Or he can enter a living body, and hold that man's mind and organs in check, and for the time being act thru the body of that man. That is done by the Yogi coming to this discrimination of Purusha and nature. If he wants to enter another's body he makes a Samyama on that body and enters it, because, not only is his Soul omnipresent, but his mind also, as the Yogi teaches. It is one bit of the universal mind. Now, however, it can only work thru the nerve currents in this body, but when the Yogi has loosened himself from these nerve currents, he can work thru other things.

41—By the conquest of the current Samana he is surrounded by a blaze of light.

Whenever he likes light flashes from his body. —

42—By making Samyama on the relation between the ear and the Akasa comes divine hearing.

There is the Akasa, the ether, and the instrument, the ear. By making Samyama on them the Yogi gets supernormal hearing; he hears everything. Anything spoken or sounded miles away he can hear.

43—By making Samyama on the relation between the Akasa and the body and becoming light as cotton-wool, etc., through meditation on them, the Yogi goes through the skies.

This Akasa is the material of this body; it is only Akasa in a certain form that has become the body. If the Yogi makes a Samyama on this Akasa material of his body, it acquires the lightness of Akasa, and he can go anywhere through the air. So in the other case also.

44—By making Samyama on the 'real modification' of the mind, outside of body, called great this disembodiedness, comes disappearance of the covering to light.

The mind in its foolishness thinks that it is working in this body. Why should I be bound by one system of nerves, and put the Ego only in one body, if the mind is omnipresent? There is no reason why I should. The YOGI wants to feel the Ego wherever he likes. The mental waves which arise in the absence of egoism in the body are called 'real modifications' or 'great disembodiedness.' When he has succeeded in making SAMYAMA on these modifications, all covering to light goes away, and all darkness and ignorance vanish. Everything appears to him to be full of knowledge.

45. By making Samyama on the gross and fine forms of the elements, their essential traits, the inherence of the Gunas in them and on their contributing to the experience of the soul, comes mastery of the elements.

46—From that comes minuteness, and the rest of the powers, 'glorification of the body' and indestructibleness of the bodily qualities.

This means that the Yogi has attained the eight powers. He can make himself as minute as a particle, or as huge as a mountain, as heavy as the earth, or as light as the air; he can reach anything he likes, he can rule everything he wants, he can conquer everything he wants, and so on. A lion will sit at his feet like a lamb, and all his desires be fulfilled at will.

47—The 'glorification of the body' is beauty, complexion, strength, admantine hardness.

The body becomes indestructible. Nothing can injure it. Nothing can destroy it until the Yogi wishes. "Breaking the rod of time he lives in this universe with his body". In the Vedas it is written that for that man there is no more disease, death or pain.

52—The Yogi should not feel allured or

flattered by the overtures of celestial beings, for fear of evil again.

There are other dangers too; gods and other beings come to tempt the Yogi. They do not want anyone to be perfectly free. They are jealous, just as we are, and worse than us sometimes. They are very much afraid of losing their places. Those Yogis who do not reach perfection die and become gods; leaving the direct road they go into one of the side streets, and get these powers. Then again they have to be born; but he who is strong enough to withstand these temptations, and go straight to the goal, becomes free.

1—The Siddhis (powers) are attained by birth, chemical means, power of words, mortification or concentration.

Sometimes a man is born with the Siddhis, powers, of course those he had earned in his previous incarnation. This time he is born, as it were, to enjoy the fruits of them. It is said of Kapila, the great father of the Sankhya Philosophy, that he was a born Siddha, which means, literally, a man who has attained to success.

The Yogis claim that these powers can be gained by chemical means. All of you know that chemistry originally began as alchemy; men went in search of the philosopher's stone and elixirs of life, and so forth. In India there was a sect called the Rasayanas. Their idea was that ideality, knowledge, spirituality and religion, were all very right, but that the body was the only instrument by which to attain to all these. If the body came to an end every now and again it would take so much more time to attain to the goal. For instance, a man wants to practice Yoga, or wants to become spiritual. Before he has advanced very far he dies. Then he takes another body and begins again, then dies, and so on. In this way much time will be lost in dying and being born again. If the body could be made strong and perfect, so that it would get rid of birth and death, we should have so much more time to become spiritual. So these Rasayanas say, first make the body very strong. They claim that this body can be made immortal. Their idea is that if the mind manufactures the body, and if it be true that each mind is only one outlet to the infinite energy, there should be no limit to each outlet getting any amount of power from outside. Why is it impossible to keep our bodies all the time? We have to manufacture all the bodies that we ever have. As soon as this body dies we shall have to manufacture another. If we can do that, why cannot we do it just here and now, without getting out of the present body? The theory is perfectly correct. If it is possible that we live after death, and make other bodies, why is it impossible that we should have the power of making bodies here, without entirely dissolving this body, simply changing it continually? They also thought that in mercury and in sulphur was hidden the most wonderful power, and that by certain preparations of these a man could keep the body as long as he liked. Others believed that certain drugs could bring powers, such as flying thru the air. Many of the most wonderful medicines of the present day we owe to the Rasayanas, notably the use of metals in medicine. Certain sects of Yogis claim that many of their principal teachers are still living in their old bodies. Pantajali, the great authority on Yoga, does not deny this.

From the Mayavati Memorial Edition.

For more of this read Raja Yoga, by Swami Vivekananda.

Introduction To
LALITA SAHASRANAMA.
- The Mother of the Universe -

This is the work of Sri Bhaskararaya. I have translated it for the Truth Seeker, as it is very highly respected by all devotees of the Kundalini, The Mother of the Universe. It is the best japa to please the Mother of the Universe. All Mantras are hidden in this japa, the fulfilment of all desires. The sick have been healed by only reading it, the poor have attained wealth, and fears have been removed. "To obtain the favor of the Mother of the Universe, one should repeat the Thousand Names."

"He who recites my Thousand Names once, is my devotee. He shall be known as dear to me, and I will give him all that he desires when having worshipped me in the Sir Chakras."

The Vyu Purana says: "One should repeat Devi's names on the water, in the forest, on the land, and any place where fear arises from wild animals or thieves. The names of Devi's should be repeated always, for such a one will be liberated from himself and bondage."

The Kebika Purana says: "O Mother of the Universe, those who praise Thee by words,—Ambika, Jaganmaya and Maya will obtain All."

"The Vandika and Tantrika rites of repeating once the Thousand Names are better than bathing in the Holy Ganges, or other places."

For the purification of oneself and fulfilment of desires, repeat the Thousand Names.

Swami Vivekananda, wrote in his book Raja Yoga, about, 'The power of words.' "There are certain sacred words called Mantrams, which have power, when repeated under proper conditions, to produce these extraordinary powers. We are living in the midst of such a mass of miracles, day and night, that we do not think anything of them. There is no limit to man's power, the power of words and the power of mind."

The reader will find these Thousand sayings, like the Upanishads teachings, beginning from Gross to Subtle and more Subtle Truth. The repetition of many words will be found here but these are most important.

Author — May 10, 1930.

THE BHAGAVATI: MOTHER KUNDALINI.

The Thousand Names

1. The Holy Mother.
2. The Great Queen.
3. The Ruler of the Highest Throne.
4. Thou art born from the Altar of Fire (dispeller of ignorance and darkness).
5. Thou art manifested for the seeker of Devas (to kill the Asura darkness).
6. Thou shineth greater than a thousand suns.
7. Thou hast four arms.
8. Thou holdest the noose of desire.
9. Thou shinest with the elephant hook of wrath and knowledge (she is both hatred and worldly knowledge).
10. Thou art armed with the bow of mind (lower and higher).
11. Thou art the arrow of the five elements.
12. Thou sprinklest the whole Universe with its rose effulgence.
13. Thy hair is adorned with the Champaka flowers.
14. Thy crown is made of gems.

15. Thy forehead shines like the Moon of the Eighth day.

16. Thou art the spot of Kasturi as the moon.

17. Thy eyebrows are like arches.

18. Thy eyes are most beautiful.

19. Thy nose is like the beautiful Champaka flower.

20. The jewel on Thy nose shineth like the stars.

21. The Kadamba flowers are worn on Thy ears.

22. Thy two rings are the Sun and Moon.

23. Thy cheeks are brighter than the ruby.

24. Thy lips are brighter than the red-cherries.

25. Thy teeth shine like wisdom.

26. The betel is in Thy mouth.

27. Thy sweet speech is golden.

28. With Thy sweet smile all are over-powered.

29. There is no other chin like Thine.

30. Thou hast a thread like a marriage vow around Thy neck.

31. The golden ornaments are on Thy arms.

32. Thou hast a necklace of pearls, gems and gold.

33. Thy two breasts are like two fruits.

34. Thy two breasts are like the most beautiful of gems.

35. Thy waist is most beautiful.

36. There is a golden belt about Thy waist.

37. Thou hast shining, rose tinted garments.

38. Thy garments are laden with gems.

39. Thy thighs are adorable and exquisitely beautiful.

40. Thou hast delightful knees.

41. Thou hast the most lovely calves.

42. Thy ankles are beautifully rounded.

43. Thou art possessed with an instep arched like a tortoise back.

44. Rays of brightness from Thy nails dispell darkness of Thy worshippers.

45. The soles of Thy feet are most beautiful.

46. Thou hast Lotus feet.

47. Thy walk is like a swan.

48. Thou art the Beauty of the Beautiful.

49. Thou art all rosy.

50. Thou hast a faultless body.

51. Thou hast every ornament.

52. Thou sittest on the lap of Siva.

53. Thou art Omnipresent.

54. Thou art the Giver of Happiness and Liberation.

55. Thou livest in the middle peak of Mount Sumeru (the Gold Mountain).

56. Thou art the Ruler of the Beautiful City.

57. Thou livest in the house made of Lucky Stones.

58. Thou sittest on the seat Formed by Five Brahmas.

59. Thou resideth in the great forest of Lotuses (symbol of Chakras).

60. Thou livest in the garden of Kadamba trees.

61. Thou livest in the center of the Ocean of Nectar.

62. Thou art lovely-eyed.

63. Thou art the Fulfiller of Desires.

64. Devas and Rishis praise Thy powers.

65. Thou art the Master of Power.

66. Thou art attended by herds of Deities.

67. Thou art surrounded by many million Goddesses.

68. Thou are seated on the Chariot and armed with all Power.

69. Thou art attended by Mantriui (a Deity).

70. Thou art preceded by Dandanatha and other Goddesses.

71. Thou resideth in the fortress of the bodies.

72. Thou art pleased at the action of Shaktis that destroy ignorance.

73. Thou art pleased to see the rising of the Nityas (the fifteen Devatas).

74. Thou gladden in the power of Bala (who killed the evil doer).

75. Thou art delighted at the destruction of Vishanga.

76. Thou art pleased at the power of Varahi.

77. Sri Ganesvara was formed by Thy glances.

78. When Ganesa broke the obstacle of the magic, Thou wast delighted.

79. Thou dischargeth Missele to answer the Bhandasura (realization of self and overcoming ignorance).

80. From Thy nails the ten Vishnu take form.

81. From Thy third eye Thou burn the arms of Daitya (the mental modification that gives birth to ignorance).

82. Thou with Thy power burned all the

army of Bhandasura (Bhandasura is the cause of duality).

83. Thy pleasure is by Brahma (Creator), Vishnu (Keeper), Mahendra (Deities).

84. Thou giveth life to Manmatha (who was burned by the fire of Siva's third eye).

85. Thy face represents the Divinity.

86. From throat to waist Thou represents the desire of Creation.

87. From thy waist downward Thou represents the Shakti.

88. Thou art the root of all Mantras.

89. Thy body is the form of three Mantras.

90. Thou art the taste of Nectar.

91. Thou art the Protector of the Family.

92. Thou art the Family Woman.

93. Thou art in the Kula (Knowledge).

94. Thou belongeth to Kula.

95. Kulayogini (Thou unitest the Chakras with Yoga).

96. Thou hast no Kula (Thou art above the Powers).

97. Thou liveth in the Samaya.

98. Thou art devoted to the conduct of Samaya, (who awakes her).

99. Thou resideth in the Muladhara (Chakra).

100. Thou severeth the Knot (open the Chakra).

101. Thou openeth the Vishugaranthi.

102. Thou appeareth in the Manipura Chakra.

103. Thou openeth the Rudragranthi (the Anahata Chakra).

104. Thou goest to Ajna Chakra.

105. Thou reacheth the Thousand Petals.

106. Thou showereth down the Ambrosia.

107. Thou art brighter than the flash of lightning.

108. Thou resideth above the Six Chakras.

109. Thou art attached to Siva.

110. Thou art Kundalini.

111. Thou art Finer than the fiber of the Lotus stalk.

112. Thou art Bhavani (Giver of Life).

113. Thou canst be attained by Meditation.

114. Thou art the Woodcutter of the forest of earthly existence.

115. Thou delighteth in Benevolence.

116. Thou art of Benevolent Appearance.

117. Thou art the Giver of Prosperity to Thy devotees.

118. Thou art pleased by Devotion.

119. Thou canst be reached by Devotion.

120. Thou art controlled by Devotion.

121. Thou art the Dispeller of Fear.

122. Thou art Sambhavi (Mudra also can be Mother of the devotees).

123. Thou art worshipped by Sarada (the Deities of Speech).

124. Thou art Sarvani.

125. Thou art the Giver of Happiness.

126. Thou art Sankari (a state of consciousness known to Yogis).

127. Thou art the Giver of Success.

128. Thou art above the Past, the Present and the Future.

129. Thy face is like the Spring Moon.

130. Thou art slender waisted.

131. Thou art Peaceful.

132. Thou art not Dependent on any but Support all.

133. Thou art Stainless.

134. Thou art Pure.

135 Thou art Spotless.

136. Thou art the Eternal.

137. Thou art Formless.

138. Thou art Ever Calm.

139. Thou art without quality (above all).

140. Thou art Partless.

141. Thou art the State of Tranquility.

142. Thou art Desirableness.

143. Thou art Indestructible.

144. Thou art Ever Free.

145. Thou art Changless.

146. Thou art Extentionless.

147. Thou art Bodiless.

148. Thou art Ever Pure.

149. Thou art Ever Wise.

150. Thou art Blameless.

151. Thou art the Compact.

152. Thou art Causeless.

153. Thou art Faultless.

154. Thou art without Limitation.

155. Thou art without Superior.

156. Thou art Passionless.

157. Thou art the Destroyer of attachments or lower desire.

158. Thou art Prideless.

159. Thou art the Killer of Pride.

160. Thou art without Care.

161. Thou art without Egoism.

162. Thou art without Bewilderment.
163. Thou art the Killer of Bewilderment.
164. Thou art Disinterestedness.
165. Thou art the Killer of Selfishness.
166. Thou art without Sin.
167. Thou art the Destroyer of Sin.
168. Thou art above Anger.
169. Thou overcometh Anger.
170. Thou art Greedless.
171. Thou art the Destroyer of Greed.
172. Thou art without Doubt.
173. Thou art the Destroyer of Doubt.
174. Thou art without Origin.
175. Thou art the Destroyer of Samsara (the cause of the misery of the people of this world).
176. Thou art without a fault.
177. Thou art undisturbed (because above the illusion).
178. Thou art Difference-less.
179. Thou art the Destroyer of Difference.
180. Thou art Imperishable.
181. Thou art the Destroyer of Death (Giver of Immortality.).
182. Thou art Actionless.

183. Thou receiveth nothing.
184. Thou art Incomparable.
185. Thou art blue-haired.
186. Thou wilt not perish.
187. Thou art without transgression.
188. Thou art difficult to attain.
189. Thou art difficult to approach.
190. Thou art a Durga (Goddess).
191. Thou art the Destroyer of Pain.
192. Thou art the Giver of Happiness.
193. Thou art unattainable by ignorant.
194. Thou puttest an End to evil.
195. Thou art above Love, Hate. etc.
196. Thou art Omnipresent.
197. Thou art Intense Compassion.
198. Thou art Above all Else.
199. Thou possesseth all Shaktis (powers).
200 Thou art the Source of All.
201. Thou art the Way to the Right Path.
202. Thou art the Ruler of All.
203. Thou art All.
204. Thou art the Essence of all Mantras.
205. Thou art the Soul of all Yantras.
206. Thou art the Spirit of all Tantras.
207. Thou art Manonmani (the Shakti of Siva).

208. Thou art Mahasvari (The Supreme).

209. Thou art Mahadevi (Great Goddess).

210. Thou art Mahalakshami (Greatest Goddess of Wealth).

211. Thou art the Beloved of Mrida (The Maker of Happiness).

212. Thou art the Great Shape.

213. Thou art the Mighty Object of Worship.

214. Thou art the Destroyer of Crime.

215. Thou art Mahamaya (Great Illusion).

216. Thou art the Great Reality.

217. Thou art the Great Energy.

218. Thou art the Great Delight.

219. Thou art the Great Extension.

220. Thou art the Great Ruler.

221. Thou art the Great Strength.

222. Thou art the Almighty.

223. Thou art the Great Intelligence.

224. Thou art the Great Attainment.

225. Thou art the Ruler of the Great Ruler.

226. Thou art the Great Tantra.

227. Thou art the Great Mantra.

228. Thou art the Great Yantra.

229. Thou art the Great Asan (Posture).

230. Thou art the Worship of Mahagaga (Great Secret).

231. Thou art Worshipped by Maha-bhairava (the Creator, Preserver and Des-troyer.

232. Thou art witness to the Great Cycle.

233. Thou art the Wife of Mahakavas-vara.

234. Thou art the Great Tripurasundari (the city of Three).

235. Thou art to be adorned by Sixty-four Ceremonies (worshipped by all).

236. Thou art Sixty-four Sciences.

237. Thou art attended by Six Hundred and Forty million Yogis.

238. Thou art Manu Vidya (Knowled-ge).

239. Thou art Chandar Vidya, (Wisdom of the Moon).

240. Thou art residing in the Moon Cen-ter (She goes to Second Chakra).

241. Thou art the Most Beautiful.

242. Thou art with the Most Beauti-ful Smile..

243. Thou art the Beautiful Moon (in the

form of Consciousness).

244. Thou art Ruler of All Worlds.

245. Thou resideth in the Six Chakras.

246. Thou art Parvati (daughter of the Himalaya).

247. Thou art Lotus-eyed.

248. Thou art Light of Light.

249. Thou art Seated on the seat of Five Forms.

250. Thou art the Five Brahmas.

251. Thou art Consciousness.

252. Thou art the Bliss of Bliss.

253. Thou art the Essence of Consciousness.

254. Thou art the Meditator and the Meditation.

255. Thou art above Virtue and Vice.

256. Thou art Omnipresent.

257. Thou art the Waking State.

258. Thou art the Dreaming State.

259. Thou art the Conscious State.

260. Thou art the Sleeping State.

261. Thou art the Knower of All.

262. Thou art the State of Ecstacy.

263. Thou art the All Transending State.

264. Thou art the Creator.

265. Thou art in the Form of Brahma.

266. Thou art the Protector.

267. Thou art in the Form of Vishnu.

268. Thou art the Destroyer.

269 Thou art in the Form of Rudra.

270. Thou art the Ever-invisible.

271. Thou art the Isvari (Ruler).

272. Thou art the Sada Siva.

273. Thou art the Giver of Bliss.

274. Thou art devoted to the five factions.

275. Thou art residing in the Sun (Third Chakra).

276. Thou art Bhairavi (who takes the form—some times Siva, other time Devi).

277. Thou hast a Garland of Prosperity.

278. Thou art seated on the Lotus (Padmasan).

279. Thou art Bhagaveti (the Source of all Goodness).

280. Thou art the Sister of Vishnu.

281. At Thy Command all worlds appear and disappear.

282. Thou hast unlimited Heads and Faces.

283. Thou hast unlimited Eyes.

284. Thou art Infinite footed.

285. Thou art the Mother of All, —from worm to Brahma.

286. Thou hast Established All.

287. The Vedas are the expression of Thy Command.

288.–Thou art the Giver of all Results.

289. All is formed from Thy Self.

290. Thou art enclosed in the shell (Om comes from shell–a symbol).

291. Thou art the Fulfillment of all Men.

292. Thou art the Fullness.

293. Thou art the Enjoyer.

294. Thou art the Ruler of the Universe.

295. Thou art the Mother.

296. Thou art without Beginning or End.

297. Thou art attended by all deities (Brahma).

298. Thou art Narayani.

299. Thou art in the Sound.

300. Thou art above Name and Form.

301. Thy syllable Hrim (is a symbol word; Hrim has been used for purposely con trolling the Three).

302. Thou art possession of Hrim.

303. Thou resideth in the Heart.

304. Thou hast no regret–Thou dost not receive.

305. Thou art worshipped by Rajaraja.

306. Thou art the Queen of the Universe.

307. Thou art the Beautiful One.

308. Thou hast eyes like the deer.

309. Thou delighteth everyone.

310. Thou art the Gladdener.

311. Thou shouldst be tasted.

312. Thou art covered with Gold.

313. Thou art Rama.

314. Thy face is like a Full Moon.

315. Thou art in the form of Sita (Holy woman).

316. Thou art the Beloved of Sita.

317. Thou art the Protector.

318. Thou art the Slayer of Rakshassas (A human being in wild state).

319. Thou art Woman.

320. Thou art the Devoted of Husbands.

321. Thou art the Desired of All.

322. Thou art in the forms of Siva and Shakti.

323. Thou art fond of Flowers.

324. Thou art Beneficient.

325. Thou art the Root of the World.

326. Thou art Compassion (like as the ocean).

327. Thou art the Possessor of all Sciences.

328. Thou art in the Science.

329. Thou art Beautiful.

330. Thou art fond of Mead.

331. Thou art the Giver of Boons.

332. O Beautiful-Eyed!

333. Thou art disturbed by liquor.

334. Thou transendest the Universe.

335. Thou canst be known thru the Vedas (Holy book of Wisdom).

336. Thou art living in the Vindhya Mountain.

337. Thou art the Supporter of All.

338. Thou art Mother.

339. Thou art Maya of Vishnu.

340. Thou art playful.

341. Thy Body is the Matter.

342. Thou art the Ruler of Matter.

343. Thou art the Protector of Matter.

344. Thou art free from Old age and Decay.

345. Thou art worshiped by Kshetrapala.

346. Thou art the Knowledge Itself.

347. Thou art Spotless.

348. Thou art Worthy of love.

349. Thou art fond of the Devotee.

350. Thou art the Speaker of the Word.

351. O Beautiful - Haired!

352. Thou art in the Fire.

353. Thou art the Kalpa Creeper of the Bhaktas (the Kalpa Creeper yields everything desired).

354. Thou freeth the Ignorant from

Bondage.

355. Thou art the Destroyer of Heretics.

356. Thou leadeth to right Action.

357. Thou art the Moon to protect those who are burning with the Fire of Misery.

358. Thou art ever the Same.

359. Thou art worshiped by the Wise.

360. O slender-Waisted!

361. Thou art the Giver of Light.

362. Thou art Intelligence.

363. Thou art Tat.

364. Thou art Essence of Intelligence.

365. Thou art Bliss of Brahma.

366. Thou art Para.

367. Thou art the Inner Consciousness.

368. Thou canst see All in Thyself.

369. Thou art the Supreme Deity.

370. Thou art the Middle (or Middle Path).

371. Thou art in the form of Vikhari.

372. Thou art the Swan of Bhakta.

373. Thou art the Vital Force.

374. Thou art the Judge above All.

375. Thou art worshipped by Kama.

376. Thou art the Essence of Love.

377. Thou art Victorious.

378. Thou art residing in the Jalandhara.

379. Thou art remaining in the center called Odhyana.

380. Thou art abiding in the Bindu.

381. Thou art to be worshipped in all sacrificial rites.

382. Thou art pleased in the offering.

383. Thou art the giver of Grace.

384. Thou art the witness of the Universe.

385. Thou art not seen by Any.

386. Thou art accompained by Deities.

387. Thou art the Possessor of the Six Qualities.

388. Thou art Ever Compassionate.

389. No one is equal to Thee.

390. Thou art the Giver of Nirvana.

391. Thou art the Sixteen Eternal Deities.

392. Thou possesseth the half-body of Siva.

393. Thou art the Giver of Light.

394. Thou art the form of Brightness.

395. Thou art Celibate.

396. Thou art the Supreme Ruler.

397. Thou art the First Cause.

398. Thou art the Unmanifested.

399. Thou art the Manifested.

400 Thou art All-Pervading.

401. Thou possesseth All Forms

402. Thou art Knowledge and Ignorance.

403. Thou art the Moonlight which gladdens the flower Kumuda.

404 Thou art the Sunbeam that gives light to Bhakta.

405. Thou art worshipped by Siva.

406. Thou art in the form of Siva.

407. Siva is Thy messenger.

408. Thou art the Giver of Happiness.

409. Thou art the Beloved of Siva.

410 Thou art beyond Siva.

411. Thou art desired by the Wise.

412. Thou art worshipped by the Great One.

413. Thou canst not be measured.

414. Thou art Self-light.

415. Thou art beyond the reach of Mind and Speech.

416. Thou art the Power of the Mind.

417. Thou art in the form of Consciousness.

418. Thou art the energy of the Inanimate Creation (Power of Vishnu or Maya).

419. Thou art the object of the World.

420. Thou art Gayatiti (Mother of Vedas or Holy Woman).

421. Thou art Vyahritih (A Mantra).

422. Thou art Sandhya (morning and

evening junction time or meditation. Also
means Brahma).

423. Thou art worshiped by all the Twi-
ce-born.

424. Thou art Asana Thy seat.

425. Thou art Tat (That).

426. Thou art Tavam (Thou).

427. Thou art Asi (Art).

428. Thou art residing in the Five Bodies.

429. Thou canst not be Bounded.

430. Thou art ever young.

431. Thou art shining (brilliantly).

432. Thy eyes roll (away from worldly
things).

433. Thou art with rose-colored Cheeks.

434. Thy body is smeared with Sandal
wood.

435. Thou art fond of flowers.

436. Thou art Skillful.

437. Thou art Graceful.

438. Thou art in the Sir Chakras.

439. Thou art of the Tried.

440. Thou art abiding in the Bindu (Muladhara).

441. Thou art worshipped by Devotees.

442. Thou art Mother of Ganesa.

443. Thou art Contentment.

444. Thou art Nourishment.

445. Thou art Intelligence.

446. Thou art Dhritah (which **gives** strength–calmness to endure pain).

447. Thou art Tranquility.

448. Thou art ever True.

449. Thou art shining resplendent.

450. Thou art Daughter of Nanda.

451. Thou art destroyer of Obstacles.

452. Thou art the support of the Sun.

453. Thou art Three-eyed (Fire, Moon and Sun).

454. Thou art the desire of women.

455. Thou art Garlanded.

456. Thou art a Swan (wise).

457. Thou art our Mother.

458. Thou art in the Himalayas.

459. O Beautiful-faced!

460. Thou art the Lotus.

461. Thou hast beautiful Eyebrows.

462. Thou art **Handsome.**

463. Thou art Leader of Devas.

464. Thou art Wife of Siva

465. Thou art **Radiant.**

466. Thou art the cause of Motion.

467. Thou art in the Finer **Form.**

468. Thou art Deity of Jalandhara.

469. Thou art Vamadevi (worshipped by all).

470. Thou art above Childhood, Youth, Old age, etc.

471. Thou art the Ruler of Sidhas.

472. Thou art the Sciences of Sidha.

473. Thou art Mother of Sidha.

474. Thou art Famous.

475. Thou art abiding in the Visudha Chakra.

476. O Rosy Color!

477. Thou art Three-eyed.

478. Thou art armed with the Club, etc.

479. Thou art One-Faced.

480. Thou art fond of Milk.

481. Thou art Deity of Feeling.

482. Thou inspirest fear in the Ignorant.

483. Thou art surrounded by other Powers.

484. Thou art the Nine Attributes.

485. Thou art in the Anahata Chakra.

486. Thou art the Black Color.

488. Thou art with Tusks.

487. Thou art Two-faced.

489. Thou weareth the Aksha beads.

490. Thou art in the Blood.

491. Thou art attended by All Power.

492. Thou art lover of Oily Foods.

493. Thou art giving Boons to Bliss.

494. Thou art Mother Rakini.

495. Thou stayest in the Manipura.

696. Thou art Three-faced.

497. Thou art armed with Thunderbolt, etc.

498. Thou art attended by Damari.

499. Thou art Raktauarni (blood color).

500. Thou art the Ruler of Flesh.

501. Thou giveth happiness to all Thy devotees.

502. Thou art fond of Sweets.

503. Thou assumeth the form of Mother Lakini.

504. Thou art in the Svadhisthana Chakra.

505. Thou art Four-faced. (Charming).

506. Thou art armed with Weapons.

507. Thou art Yellow.

508. Thou art Splendid.

509. Thou art Ruler over Fat.

510. Thou art fond of Honey.

511. Thou art attended by Bandhini (one of the six deities).

512. Thou art fond of Curd.

513. Thou assumeth the form of Kakini.

514. Thou art climbing to the Muladhara Chakra.

515. Thou art Five-faced.

516. Thou art the Ruler over the Bones.

517. Thou hast Power with the elephant hook.

518. Thou art attended by Varada and others.

519. Thou art fond of Food.

520. Thou assumeth the form of Sakani.

521. Thou resideth over the Ajna Chakra.

522. Thou art White (pure).

523. Thou art Six-faced.

524. Thou art Ruler of the Marrow.

525. Thou art attended by Hamsavati and others.

526. Thou art fond of Flavored Foods.

527. Thou taketh the Hakini form.

528. Thou resideth in the Thousand-Petaled Lotus.

529. Thou shineth with colors.

530. Thou hast all weapons.

531. Thou art in the Semen.

532. Thou art facing Everywhere.

533. Thou art in all Foods.

534. Thou art taking the form of Mother Yakini.

535. Thou art Svaha.

536. Thou art Svadha.

537. Thou art Non-intelligence.

538. Thou art Intelligence.

539. Thou art Srutih (Scriptures).

540. Thou art Smrithih.

541. Thou art the Best.

542. Thou art Righteousness.

543. Thou canst be attained by Righteousness.

544. Thou heareth the praises of the Holy Three.

545. Thou art worshiped by Indra's wife.

546 Thou freeth the Ignorant.

547. Thou art Wavy haired.

548. Thou art Parabrahama (God).

549. Thou art Wisdom.

550. Thou art the Mother of the Universe, Ether, etc.

551. Thou art the cure of all Disease.

552. Thou art dispelling all Death.

553. Thou art the First.

554. Thou art Unthinkable.

555. Thou art the destroyer of Sin.

556. Thou art daughter of the Rishi Kata.

557. Thou art the destroyer of Time.

558. Thou art worshipped by Vishnu (the Preserver).

559. Thou hold the betel in Thy mouth.

560. Thou art the hue of many Flowers.

561. Thou art Fawn-eyed.

562. Thou art Fascinating.

563. Thou art the First Born of Truth.

564. Thou art Maridani (the Giver of Happiness).

565. Thou art The Friend.

566. Thou art Eternal Bliss.

567. Thou hast fulfilled the desires of Bhaktas.

568. Thou art The Guide.

569. Thou art the Ruler of All.

570. Thou can be attained by Cheerfulness.

571. Thou art the witness of the dissolution of the Universe.

572. Thou art perfect Eenrgy.

573. Thou art pefect Endlessness.

574. Thou art pure Wisdom.

575. Thou art the Essence of Wine.

576. Thou art Enthusiasm.

577. Thou art in the form of A.

578. Thou art in the Kailasa (Holy of the Holy.)

579. Thou hast soft arms.

580. Thou art Illustrious.

581. Thou art Mercy.

582. Thou art holding the Wide Dominion.

583. Thou art Atmavidya (wisdom of the self.

584. Thou art the Science of Aspiration.

585. Thou art the Sacred Science.

586. Thou art attended by the God of Love.

587. Thou art the Science of the Sixteen Syllables.

588. Thou art Three-peaked.

589. Thou art the Spirit of Kama.

590. Thou art attended by Millions.

591. Thou art in the Head.

592. Thou art Moon-like.

593. Thou art in the Forehead.

594. Thou art of the Rainbow Color.

595. Thou art in the Heart.

596. Thou art Sun-like.

597. Thou art light in the Triangle.

598. Thou art Daughter of Daksha or Wife of Siva.

599. Thou art killer of Datyas.

601. Thou art Destroyer of Daksha's sacrifice.

600. Thou art within the Large Eyes.

602. Thou art The Within—whose face shines with a smile.

603. Thou art in the form of Teacher.

604. Thou art All Qualities.

605. Thou art Mother of the Cow.

606. Thou art Mother of Guha.

607. Thou art Ruler of Gods.

608. Thou art in Justice.

609. Thou art Brahma in the Heart.

610. Thou art worshipped fifteen days of the Full Moon.

611. Thou art in the Kala. (12 Suns, 16 Moons, etc).

612. Thou art Ruler of Kala, etc.

613. Thou art the Speech of the Poets.

614. Thou art attended by Lakshami and Saraswati (Goddess' of Wealth and Wisdom).

615. Thou art the First Energy.

616. Thou art Immeasurable.

617. Thou art Atma.

618. Thou art the Supreme.

619 Thou art the pure One.

620. Thou art Creator of the many millions of worlds.

621. Thou art divinely Formed.

622. Thou art the Klim. (Other name of Siva).

623. Thou art the Absolute.

624. Thou art the Secret.

625. Thou art bestower of the Fifth State of Consciousness.

626. Thou art older than the Three.

627. Thou art worshipped by the Three Worlds.

628. Thou art in the (Three) Forms.

629. Thou art Ruler of the Thrice–Ten.

630. Thou art in the Three syllabled.

631. Thou art the divine Perfume.

632. Thou hast the Red Forehead Mark.

633. Thou art Uma.

634. Thou art Daughter of the Mountain King.

635. Thou art Gauri (yellow).

636. Thou art attended by Gandharvas.

637. Thou containest all the Universe in Thyself.

638. Thou art born from the Golden.

639. Thou art the Punisher of the Fool.

640. Thou art the Ruler of Speech.

641. Thou art attained by Meditation.

642. Thou art the Unlimited.

644. Thou art the Embodiment of Knowledge.

643. Thou art the Giver of Knowledge.

645. Thou canst be known thru the Vadanta. (Wisdom.)

646. Thou art Truth and Bliss.

647. Thou art worshiped by Lopamudra.

648. Thou hast created the world system as it were, in sport.

649. Thou art Invisible.

650. Thou art above the Visible.

651. Thou art the Perceiver.

652. Thou art transcending all Knowledge.

653. Thou art Yogini.

654. Thou art Bestower of Yoga.

655. Thou art Yoga.

656. Thou art the Bliss of Yoga.

657. Thou supportest the Universe.

658. Thou art the Desire, the Action and the Wisdom.

659. Thou art the Supporter of All.

660. Thou art firmly Established.

661. Thou art the Foundation of Truth and Untruth.

662. Thou art Eight-Formed,

663. Thou art Conquerer of Ignorance.

664. Thou art the Director of the Worlds.

665. Thou art One.

666. Thou holdeth all things together.

667. Thou art Non-duality.

668. Thou art above Duality.

669. Thou art the Giver of Food.

670. Thou art the Giver of Wealth.

671. Thou art the ancient Om.

672. Thou unitest the Atma to Brahma.

673. Thou art Great.

674. Thou art Brahmani (Divine Wisdom).

675. Thou art Brahmi; female part of Brahma.

676. Thou art the Bliss of Brahma.

677. Thou art the Enjoyment in the Mighty.

678. Thou art in all Languages.

679. Thou art with the mighty Army.

680. Thou art above Existence and Non-existence.

681. Thou art very easily Worshipable.

682. Thou doeth good to the Worshiper.

683. Thou art the Right means and not hard to attain.

684. Thou art the King of Kings.

685. Thou art the Giver of Dominon.

686. Thou art the Spirit of Gladness in Dominion. (in the six Chakras).

687. Thou art Compassionate.

688. Thou art the Supporter of all Kings.

689. Thou art their Wealth.

690. Thou art the Ruler of all Treasures.

691. Thou art the Commander of all Armies.

692. Thou art the Giver of Samrajya (the sacrifice by the King of Kings).

693. Thou art devoted to Truth.

694. Thou art girdled by the Ocean.

695. Thou art the Initiator.

696. Thou art the Controller of all Daityas (bad doers).

697. Thou art the Controller of all the Worlds.

698. Thou art the fulfiller of all Desires.

699. Thou art the Creator of the Universe.

700. Thou art Satchitanandarupini (Truth, Consciousness and Bliss).

701. Thou art above Time and Space (or Force).

702. Thou art Omnipresent.

703. Thou art all Bewilderment (to the ignorant.

704. Thou art the Mother of Wisdom.

705. Thou art the Sciences.

706. Thou abidest in the Heart.

707 Thou art the Secret One.

708. Thou art free from All.

709. Thou art always with Siva.

710. Thou art the supreme of Wisdom.

711. Thou art the Well-doer.

712. Thou art I.

713. Thou art always with Gurus (spiritual teachers).

714. Thou art above the Senses.

715. Thou art worshiped in the Sun.

716. Thou art back of Maya.

717. Thou art as Honey. (or art Honeylike).

718. Thou art the Earth.

719. Thou art Mother of All.

120. Thou art worshiped by All.

721. Thou art Tender.

722. Thou art the Beloved of the Guru.

723. Thou art Independent.

724. Thou art the Ruler of the Tantras.

725. Thou art born of Siva.

726. Thou art worshiped by the Yogi.

727. Thou art the Giver of Knowledge of Siva (Siva is founder of Yoga).

728. Thou art Chitkala (Knowledge, Existence, Bliss).

729. Thou art the Gem of Bliss.

730. Thou art Affection.

731. Thou art the Cause of Affection.

732 Thou art glad in the Repetition.

733. Thou art the science of Nandi.

734. Thou art Natesvari.

735. Thou art the Root of the Illusion of the Worlds.

736. Thou art the Giver of Liberation.

737. Thou art Liberation.

738. Thou art fond of Rhythm.

739. Thou causest Absorption (a state higher than Meditation).

740. Thou art Shame.

741. Thou art adorned by Yogin.

742. Thou showereth with Nectar (rain on the world that is burning with worldly fire).

743. Thou art the First Fire to burn the Sin.

744. Thou art the Gale.

745. Thou art the beams of the Sun.

746. Thou art the beams of the Moon.

747. Thou art the Cloud (giver of spiritual rain).

748 Thou art the thunderbolt to all diseases.

749. Thou art the Axe that cuts the root of death.

750. Thou art the Mahesvari.

751. Thou art the Mahakali.

752. Thou art the Great Destroyer.

753. Thou art the Great Absorber.

754. Thou art the Great Discharger of Debt.

755. Thou art the Spirit of Anger.

756. Thou art the Devourer of all Dait-yas (who fight against gods in olden times).

757. Thou art the Perishable and the Im-perishable.

758. Thou art the Ruler of Worlds and Heaven.

759. Thou art the Supporter of the Uni-verse.

760. Thou art the Giver of Desired Ob-jects.

761. Thou art Good Fortune.

762. Thou art Three—Sun, Moon and Fire.

763. Thou art Three Qualities. – Raja, Tamas and Satva.

764. Thou art the Giver of Heaven and Liberation.

765. Thou art Pure.

766. Thou hast a form like the Rose.

767. Thou art Vitality.

768. Thou art the Bearer of Light.

769. Thou art the Sacrifice.

770. Thou art fond of Vows.

771. Thou art difficult to worship by the Uncontrolled Mind.

772. Thou art difficult to Control.

773. Thou art fond of red and white Flowers.

774. Thou art Great.

775. Thou art in the Meru (Chakra).

776. Thou art fond of Mandara Flowers.

777. Thou art worshiped by Warriors.

778. Thou art the Old Age of the warriors.

779. Thou art Passionless.

780. Thou faceth Everywhere.

781. Thou art the Interior.

782. Thou art the Highest Ether.

783. Thou art the Giver of Life.

784. Thou art the Life.

785. Thou art worshipped by Martandabharava (a Goddess above the Mental Chakra, can also be Sun).

786. Thou hast given your Kingdom to Mantrini (the protected of the Yogis).

787. Thou art Tri-puresi (the Deity).

788. Thou art the Victorious Army.

789. Thou art above Qualities.

790. Thou art the Superior and the Inferior.

791. Thou art the Truth, Wisdom and Bliss.

792. Thou art the Supreme Abode.

793. Thou art Water of the Ganges.

794. Thou art the Sixty-four Arts.

795. Thou art the Cow of Plenty (the fulfiller of desires.

796. Thou art the desire that creates the Worlds.

797. Thou art the Reservoir of Science.

798. Thou art the Poets Art.

799. Thou art the Queen of Literary Composition.

800. Thou art the Treasury of Spiritual Nectar.

801 Thou art Nourishment.

802. Thou art the Ancient or the First of All.

803. Thou art worshiped by All.

804. Thou art Lotus-faced.

805. Thou art Lotus-eyed.

806. Thou art Light of Lights.

807. Thou art the Highest Abode.

808. Thou art the Highest Atom.

809. Thou art Supreme of the Supreme.

810. Thou art holding the noose in Hand.

811. Thou art the destroyer of the Noose.

812. Thou art the Destroyer of the Hostile force.

813. Thou art finely Formed.

814. Thou art without fine Form.

815. Thou art satisfied with any Offering.

816. Thou art the Swan of the Manasa Lake.

817. Thou art the Vows of Truth.

818. Thou art Reality.

819. Thou art in every Heart.

820. Thou art Faithful Sati (the one who is ever true to her husband).

821. Thou art the Giver of life. to Brahma.

822. Thou art Brahma.

823. Thou art Mother of All.

824. Thou art manifold in Form.

825. Thou art worshiped by the Wise.

826. Thou art the Creator.

827. Fear of Thy sunshine and the fear of Thy wind.

828. Thou art the Ordinances.

829. Thou art the Foundation of All.

830. Thou ar experienced in all Forms.

831. Thou art Master of the Senses.

832. Thou art the Energy of the senses.

833. Thou art the Fifty Seats.

834. Thou art without Bondage.

835. Thou livest in the Holy place.

836. Thou art the Mother of Heroes.

837. Thou art Ether.

838. Thou art the Giver of Liberation.

839. Thou art the Home of Liberation.

840 Thou art the root of all Powers.

841. Thou art the Knower of Mind Qualities (of different states of Mind).

842. Thou art the remedy of all Diseases.

843. Thou art the Mover of the earthly wheel (she moves the world).

844. Thou art the Means to attain Wisdom.

845. Thou art the Essence of Wisdom.

846. Thou art the Essence of Mantras.

847. Thou art the Lightest of Forms.

848. Thou art the Highest Yama.

849. Thy glory is very High.

850. Thou art the Letters.

851. Thou giveth peace, birth and death to men.

852. Thou art claimed by all the Upanishads.

853. Thou art Kala (nature's finer forces).

854. Thou art Fathomless.

855. Thou art in the Ether.

856. Thou art elevated above Creation.

857. Thou art the Joy in all songs.

858. Thou art free from the world bondage.

859. Thou art the Goal of All.

860. Thou art the End of Pain and Sin.

861. Thou art the Heaven and all other Spheres.

862. Thou art above Cause and Effect.

863. Thou outflowest with Pleasure.

864. Thou wearest Golden Rings.

865. Thou takest Thy body for Fun.

866. Thou art Unborn.

867. Thou art free from Decay.

868. Thou art Beautiful.

869. Thou art easily Pleased.

870. Thou art worshiped Internally.

871. Thou art difficult to attain by the Ignorant.

872. Thou art Rig, Yojur and Saman (Revelation in Three Vedas, Holy Book of Wisdom).

873. Thou art the Object of three Desires (A. U. M. or past, present and future).

874. Thou art living in the Three.

875. Thou art Goddess of Antardasera Chakra.

87⁶. Thou art free from Disease.

877. Thou art without Support.

878. Thou art enjoying Thyself.

879. Thou art the Stream of Nectar.

880. Thou knowest how to raise Above worldly misery of those who pray to Thee.

881. Thou art fond of Sacrifice.

882. Thou performs the Sacrifice.

883. Thou art the Sacrificer.

884. Thou art the Supporter of Dharma (righteousness or right duty).

885. Thou art the Ruler of Wealth.

886. Thou increaseth Wealth.

887. Thou art fond of Knowledge.

888. Thou art manifestation of Knowledge.

889. Thou art Revolution.

890. Thou art the Absorber of All.

891. Thou art the Tree of Knowledge.

892. Thou art Mother of Vishnu.

893. Thou art in the form of Vishnu (one who preserves the world).

894. Thou art without Origin.

895. Thou art the Home of Origin.

896. Thou art the Manifestor of ignorance.

897. Thou art worshipped Externally.

898. Thou art in the assembly of Warriors.

899. Thou art Valorious.

900 Thou art above Actions.

901. Thou art in the Nada (self in the Anahata Chakra).

902. Thou art in the direct Perception.

903. Thou art Skilful.

904. Thou art Artful.

905. Thou art seated on Bindu.

906. Thou art above the Tattvas (nature's finer Forces.

907. Thou art Reality Itself.

908. Thou art the meaning of the World.

909. Thou art fond of the song of Sama Veda.

910. Thou art fit to be Worshiped.

911. Thou art the Deities.

912. Thou art in the right and left Palti.

913. Thou cleareth the Path.

914. Thou art Independent.

915. Thou art Sweet.

916. Thou art Wise.

917. Thou art worshiped by the Wise.

918. Thou art worshiped by Meditation. as Consciousness.

919. Thou art fond of Consciousness.

920. Thou art Ever Truth in the Wise.

921. Thou art Ever the Contented.

922. Thou art like the Morning Sun.

923. Thou art worshiped by the Right. and Left (wise and fool).

924. Thou wearest a sweet Smile.

925. Thou art Pure and worshipped by All.

926. Thou art Giver of Liberation.

927. Thou art fond of Praise.

928. Thou art the receiver of Praise.

929. Thou art celebrated in the Scriptures.

930. Thou art Intelligence.

931. Thou art the Higher Mind.

932. Thou art wife of Siva.

933. Thou art the Doer of Good.

934. Thou art Mother of the Universe.

935. Thou art the Supporter. of the Universe.

936. Thou art worshipped at Benare, Himalaya (between both eyes).

937. Thou art free from Passion.

938. Thou art Strong.

939. Thou art Generous.

940. Thou art highly Delightful.

941. Thou art in the Mind.

942. The ether becomes Thy hair.

943. Thou remaineth ever in the Celestial Chariot.

944. Thou art the Wife of Indra, Ruler of the World.

945. Thou art fond of Tantra.

946. Thou art fond of the Five sacrifices.

947. Thou art in the five forms, Brahma, Vishnu, Rudra, Isvara and Sadasiva.

948. Thou art The Fifth.

949. Thou art Ruler of Five.

950. Thou art worshipped with five Objects.

951. Thou art Eternal.

952. Thou art Ruler of Eternal.

953. Thou art the Giver of Happiness.

954. Thou produces confusion on the Earth.

955. Thou art the Supporter of the Earth.

956. Thou art the Daughter of the Himalayas.

957. Thou art the Possessor of Wealth.

958. Thou art Righteousness.

959. Thou art the Increaser of Righteousness.

960. Thou art above the World.

961. Thou art above the attributes.

962. Thou art above All.

963. Thou art above the World Peace.

964. Thou art Flower-like.

965. Thou art Feminine.

966. Thou art the pleased in Amusement.

967. Thou art the Seed of Success.

968. Thou giveth Happiness.

969. Thou art Beautiful.

970. Thou art the Ever Uniting One.

971. Thou art delighted by married Women.

972. Thou art Ever Beautiful.

973. Thou art Pure Minded.

974. Thou art pleased by meditation on the Bindu, (in Chakra).

975. Thou art the First Born.

976. Thou art the Deity of the Chakras.

977. Thou art worshipped by Ten Mudras.

978. Thou art Deity of the Fifth Chakras.

979. Thou art Jnanamudra.

980. Thou art to be attained by Wisdom.

981. Thou art the Wisdom and the Knowing Principle.

982. Thou art Yoni Mudra.

983. Thou art the Ruler of the Ten Mudras.

984. Thou art the Possessor of the Three Qualities.

985. Thou art the Mother.

986. Thou art in the Triangle.

987. Thou art Sinless.

988. Thy work in Wonderful.

989. Thou fullfillest desire.

990. Thou art ever known by Meditation.

991. Thou art above the Six Methods.

992. Thou art Just and Compassionate.

993. Thou art the Light that dispels the Darkness.

994. Thou art ever known to Children.

995. At Thy command, all obey.

996. Thou art residing in the Six Chakras.

997. Thou art the Divine.

998. Thou art the Divine Siva.

999. Thou art Union of Siva and Sakti.

1000. Thou art Mother Lalita, Aum (Om).

WHY WE WORSHIP SIVA

(BY UMESH CHANDRA CHAKRAVARTY)

From time immemorial the Hindus are worshipping God Siva who is master of truth, beauty and bliss. From the highest Himalayas on the north down to Rameswar in the south and from Chandranath hill on the east to Dwarka on the west the whole of India is filled up with Siva-temples here and there. So it is quite needless to give any acquaintance of God Siva to the Indians whom they are ever-familiar with. Their ins and outs are ever-filled up with the attributes of Siva and hearts ever spring with joy in His very worship! This Siva-worship is not only an object of outward form of Hindu-worship, but the Greatest Saint Acharya Sankara who perfectly realised within himself the true meaning of Indian worship of God Siva, declared quite clearly in one of the hymns called "Nirvana Shatkam" as follows:— "I am beyond all imaginations and forms, I do not obey any sense but all senses obey Me; there is nothing without Me, I am Siva Himself in the very Shape of Soul and Joy. This is the real description of Siva, the worshippers who proceed in their way with this true acquaintance of the worship-

ped are surely blessed. His worship required no particular arrangement, —He is ever
satisfied with two little prayers and offer-
ings,—a drop of water, a leaf of bel and
cheek-slap sounds only please Him the most.
We have no second thing to offer to Him,
the Atman or Soul is the only object of His
offer. In His well-known hymn of salutation we find the following expression:—
'We bow Thee down O' God, full of infinite wellfare and calmness and the root cause of
all the three worlds. I offer my soul unto
Thee. Thou God of gods and Goal
of all." Surrendering of the Self is His
only mode of worship, which trans-
form an earthly being to Divine being
full of heavenly bliss. Hence a blessed
holy person sing most loudly the highly
esteemed song "Am Siva Himself am
Siva Himself in the very shape of Soul and
Joy!"

TRUE SIGNIFICANCE

Siva worship does not require the exact
image of Siva as depicted in the hymn of
Holy Scripture, but it prefers a bright symbol of Divinity widely known as "Siva-

138

Lingam"! What is Lingam? We must
think deeply and make out its real explanation. Lingam means sign or symbol. Worship of Such Divine Symbol is a current us-
age amongst all nations of the world. The
Hindus worship Lingam, the Bouddhas,
Stupa, the Mahomedans, a Blue Stone Pulpit
in Kaba and the Christians a Cross Staff;
thus almost every great nation worships a
Divine symbol of whatever shape it may
be. The modern historians are of opinion
that the Buddhistic Stupa or Pagoda was
transformed into Siva Lingam by mighty
influence of Acharya Sankara. But actually
the worship of Siva Lingam is being
practised by the Hindus from unknown
pre-historic time. We find the origin
of its history in the last chapter of
'Dharma Samhita' of 'Siva Maha Puranam'
that when the world was totally destroyed
and there was nothing but unending flood
of water and three original representations
of Godhood namely Brahma, Vishnu and
Rudra, Brahma and Vishnu requested Rudra
most fervently for recreation of the universe. Rudra gladly consented and immersed
Himself in a long deep meditation. Some
thousand years being passed in this way and

finding no possibility of creation by Him,
Vishnu asked Brahma to perform the task,
who finished it instantly. Rudra then rose
from the meditation and finding everything
already created by Brahma, because fired
with wrath and at once attempted to destroy. At this Brahma and Vishnu came
before Him and extinguished His wrath
by entreaties, and singing long prayer in
His praise. Easily pleased He was glad-
dened instantly with that and with the
request of Brahma and others, He threw off
His fiery vigour produced through wrath
unto the Sun, who got the splendid illumin-
ation to light up the world. The Divine
Vigour of God Siva, placed thus in the Sun
is worshipped thrice a day by all as Gavatri
Savitri and Saraswati. Thereafter Siva who
secured endless life seeds for the creation
through long meditation, put off the Lingam or Symbol which is the stock of life-
seeds and threw it down on the earth. Thus
being thrown off it began to expand both
downward and upward and made unbear-
able horror to the world. Vishnu went
downward and Brahma upward to get two
ends of the same but being utterly unsuccess-
ful were staying quite unhappy. At this

moment some words were heard to be uttered in the Etherial plane that "If this blazing Symbol of Divine vigour be worshipped by all it would be pleased and the horrible temper would be transformed into broad calmness to the entire welfare of the world. By worshipping the Symbol all would worship God Siva. Thereupon all did the same whole-heartedly and happiness of the world was restored for ever and the worshippers were filled up with the spirit of Divinity and fully realised within themselves the perfect Godhood of Siva.

THREE DIVINE FORMS

From the very time of this well-known fact about the origin of Effulgent and Eternal Lingam or Symbol, the Hindus have been worshipping God Siva in Pure and Divine Symbol. Siva is not only the lord of destruction, a description in the 'Sivastakam' composed by Acharya Sankara gives out the perfectness of God Siva in three Divine forms for three divisions of work, namely Brahma as Creator, Vishnu as Supporter and Rudra as Destroyer. His symbol is ever-embraced by the Symbol of Nature, the World Mother. Here lies a very high idea of Hindu system of worship which express

as clear as daylight the true meaning of worshipping Fatherhood and Motherhood of
God symbolized together. Everyone being
the child of Father God and Mother Nature
possesses full right to worship what symbol-
ize Them both. Is it not? Yes, actually this
is the universal system of worship not at all
confined in any country, community or sect.
This is quite natural just as a child pays its
due respect to the father and mother.

In other words it is the worship of Self
or Atman and the realization of Godhood
within the worshipper himself. The spinal
column standing on the plexus which is tri-
angular in form is the symbol of that worship. From the plexus right up comes the
hollow canal called Susumna or Antara-
sunya and from the left and the right sides
come two fine nerves known as Ida and
Pingala coiled round this hollow canal or
the spinal column forming vertebra. These
are the upper end or terminus of the hollow
canal wherein to be found a mesh work
of fine nerve tissues which is on the central
part of the brain, otherwise called cerebel-
lum apart from cerebrum and medulla ob-
longata. In mythological language this
mesh or network of tissues is called the

thousand patelled lotus or Sahasrar.

This is what we find in physiological structures. Inside the hollow canal known as Susumna three concentric nerve tissues equally hollow inside are also mentioned in the book. The first or the outer one is called Vazra-naree or Indra-naree. The second one inside the first casing is called Surya-naree or Solar canal and still further inside another hollow canal mentioned is known as Brahmanaree or the hollow canal for Divinity.

SYMBOLIC DRIFT

This whole physiological representation is symbolized in stone image known as Sthanu and Gauripatta. The worshipper is to unloosen a bit of clog or small globule on the top of the Sthanu and then the worship will begin, because it is supposed that the internal passage to the higher plane is naturally blocked up which must be removed, so that the internal flow or the passage of energy might come up to the highest plane known as Sahasrar. To put in Psychological language the Atman or the Ego which is supposed to be inside the hollow canal or Susumna of the person is to be worshipped or meditated upon. From

the down plexus six stages are mentioned
as lotuses. These lotuses and stages are to
be traversed by rigid meditation upon one's
own Self and the adjoining nerve tissues of
the centre are called particular lotuses. We
have Muludhara. Swadhisthana, Manipura; Bisuddha Chakra, Anahata, Ajna
Chakra and Sahasrar. Thus worshipping
these representations one is worshipping his
Ownself or Ego. Hence no rigid ritualities
are ordained neither any caste distinction
nor speciality of persons are required. Every
person can worship Siva quite independent-
ly. It is the most non-sectarian, non-big-
oted form of worship. This worship is the
worthy self projection or super-imposition
of one's own Self or Adhyas of the Atman
as symbolized in some material casing or
stone representation.

Now in the Bamachari period when everything was explained out through the
symbol of creative agencies known as Brah-
ma-Vija and Sristhi Vija, the vertebra or
the Sthanu is called the male symbol or
Phallus of creation and the plexus or Gouripatta is called the female symbol or Phallus of production. Thus the creative aspect
of the original idea is well-preserved in the

representation which form an alter mode of explanation. The Sthanu is the representation of the Eternal column or Image known as Jyotirmoy or Effulgent Image and the Gouripatta is represented receptivity of the Divine Energy which brings forth the creation. In Common parlance it is called Firmament and Earth or Creative Father and Mother in procreation.

March 2, 1930.

From The A. B. Patrika

REV. LEADBEATER OFF THE TRAIL

The harm to Yoga philosophy that has been done by misinformation thru the "Theosophist" Rev. C. W. Leadbeater is indeed very great.

Most readers of Theosophical and Occult literature believe Rev. Leadbeater to be a friend to the Hindus, but after reading his book, "The Inner Life" and "The Chakras', I am forced to say by the information he has given, he is the greatest enemy of Yoga philosophy, and has given a bad name to Yoga. This may have been done unconsciously. Nevertheless, it is hard to believe, as in "The Chakras" he in no instance has corrected the misinformation made in "The Inner Life". For example, in "The Chakras" he tries to prove a difference in the petals of the different centers from that which is given in Yoga philosophy.

According to Rev. Leadbeater all the Yogis of the past and present, even the founder of Yoga philosophy are wrong about the Chakras, and their petals.

All Yogis and our books claim Sahasrara, has one thousand petals but in one of his

chapters, Rev. Leadbeater says he found
there were only Nine Hundred and Sixty
and not 'One Thousand'. The Ajna Chakra has two petals, according to Yoga, but
Rev. Leadbeater claims he found Ninety-six
petals in the Ajna Chakra. All his counts
are opposite the Yogis' Chakras, except one.
He claims he found Nine Hundred and Sixty
and Ninty-six.

Every Yogi cannot help but laugh, because there are really no petals at all. I will
explain here, the symbols these petals stand
for.

Every Yogi knows, and the students of
Yoga Philosophy know, that Rev. Leadbeater. is 'off the trail,' and did not stop to
consider the origin of our One Thousand Petals. but undoubtedly he had something else
in mind.

In Yoga Philosophy these Chakras are
symbols; the first—Earth, the second—Water.
third—Fire, fourth—Air, fifth—Ether and
sixth—Mental. The 'Thousand - Petaled' we
do not call a Chakra, as it is above the nature
element and mind.

In these six symbols we have the 'Garland
of Letters', as there are fifty letters in the
Sanskrit alphabet and each petal of these

centers represent a letter. In the first or Root Chakra, Yoga puts four petals, six in the second, ten in the third, twelve in the fourth, sixteen in the fifth and two in the sixth, between the eyes. That includes the occult symbol of the Sanskrit alphabet. By repreating all of the fifty alphabetical letters twenty times we have One Thousand—the symbol of the 'Thousand-petals'. We would like to know just where Rev. Leadbeater gets his idea that there are only 960. Now is he not off the trail, reader?

Now I will give you his own words about awakening the Kundalini: "One very common effect of rousing it prematurely is that it rushes downwards in the body instead of upwards, and thus excites the most undesirable passions—excites them and intensifies their effects to such a degree that it becomes impossible for the man to resist them, because a force has been brought into play, in whose presence he is as helpless as a swimmer before the jaws of a shark".

The reader will find this kind of 'stuff' in Chapter Four and in the next Chapter he contradicts as follows: "It is said in some cases Kundalini has been awakened not only by the will, but also by an accident; by a

blow or by physical pressure. I heard recently from one of our Theosophical lecturers
that he had come across an example of the
kind when touring in Canada. A lady, who
knew nothing at all of these matters fell
down the cellar steps in her house. She lay for
some time unconscious, and when she awoke
she found herself clairvoyant, able to read
the thoughts passing in other people's minds,
and to see what was going on in every room
in the house; and this clairvoyance has
remained a permanent possession. One
assumes that in this case in falling, the lady
must have received a blow at the base of
the spine exactly in such a position and of
such a nature as to shock the Kundalini into
partial activity."

The miseries and dangers spoken of in
the previous chapter, do not appear to have
been monstrous in this case.

I will now show my readers at what Rev.
Leadbeater is driving. And he does not hesi-
tate, if, at the same time he gives a bad name
to the Yoga Philosophy, because he wants
followers of his method of opening the Kundalini, and really one can hardly blame Rev.
Leadbeater, as it seems to be the custom of
the West to first give the other man a bad

name and then, seek his followers. For nearly half a century I have met Master Yogis who have awakened their Kundalini and not in a single instance did they claim they had opened it. Rev. Leadbeater is the first man to come to my attention, who claims he has opened his Kundalini. For the rest of the people he says: "but most people cannot gain it during the present incarnation, if it is the first in which they have begun to take these matters seriously in hand, but it is really for the majority, the work of a later round altogether. The conquest of the serpent-fire has to be repeated in each incarnation, since the vehicles are new each time, but after it has been once thoroughly achieved these repetitions will be an easy matter." Then on the same page he gives his own personal experience: "It may be of use if I mention my own experience in this matter. In the earlier part of my residence in India forty years ago I made no effort to rouse the fire, not indeed knowing very much about it, and having the opinion that, in order to do anything with it, it was necessary to be born with a specially psychic body, which I did not possess. But one day one of the Masters made a suggestion to me with regard to a certain kind of meditation which would evoke this force. Naturally I at once put the suggestion into practice, and in course of time was successful. I have no doubt, however, that He watched the experiment, and would have checked me if it had become dangerous. I am told that there are Indian ascetics who teach this to their pupils, of course keeping them under careful supervision during the process. But I do not my self know of any such, nor would I have confidence in them unless they were specially recommended by someone whom I knew to be possessed of real knowledge."

Rev. Leadbeater claims he has opened the Kundalini, still he will not have the confidence in the Hindu Master, unless they were specially recommended by some ghost on the Astral Plane. Following, I will show how he wants you to open the Kundalini: "People often ask me what I advise them to do with regard to the arousing of this force. I advise them to do exactly what I myself did. I recommend them to throw themselves into theosophical work and wait until they receive a definite command from some Master who will undertake to superintend their psychic development, continuing in the meantime all the ordinary exercises of meditation that are known to them. They should not care in the least whether such development comes in this incarnation or in the next, but should regard the matter from the point of view of the ego and not of the personality, feeling absolutely certain that the Masters are always watching for those whom They can help, that it is entirely impossible for anyone to be overlooked, and that They will unquestionably give Their directions when They think that the right time has come."

It would really be a great joy to all Yogis if, Rev. Leadbeater will leave the Yoga Philosophy alone and give to the world what he wants, but by all means, call it by some other name.

This is not a pleasure to me to criticise some other writer, but I believe it is the duty of every Yogi, to give to those who are seeking information, only that which he (the Yogi) knows to be correct about the Kundalini—the Mother of the Universe.

The following is an article on the same subject, by Arthur Avalon. He, too, questions Rev. Leadbeater's remarks.

From pp. 6 to 18
Mr. A. Avalon's, "The Serpent Power."

"We may here notice the account of a well-known "Theosophical" author (Mr. C. W. Leadbeater), regarding what he calls the "Force Centres" and the "Serpent Fire," of which he writes that he has had persosonal experience. Though Mr. Leadbeater also refers to the Yoga Shastra, it may perhaps exclude error if we here point out that his account does not profess to be a representation of the teaching of the Indian Yogis (whose competence for their own Yoga the author somewhat disparages), but that it is put forward as the Author's own original explanation (fortified, as he conceives, by certain portions of Indian teaching) of the personal experience which (he writes) he himself has had. This experience appears to consist in the conscious arousing of the "Serpent Fire,"[1] with the enhanced "astral" and mental vision which he believes has shown him what he tells us.[2]

1.—This and the following notes compare his and the Indian theory. The Devi or Goddess is called Bhujangi or serpent because at the lowest centre (Muladhara) she lies "coiled" round the Linga. "Coiled"—at rest. The Cosmic Power in bodies is here at rest; when roused it is felt as intense heat.

2.—Certain Siddhis or occult powers are acquired at each center as the practitioner works his way upwards.

The centres, or Chakras, of the human body are by Mr. Leadbeater described to be vortices of "etheric" matter [3] into which rush from the "astral"[4] world, and at right angles to the plane of the whirling disc, the sevenfold force of the Logos bringing "divine life" into the physical body. Though all these seven forces operate on all the centres, in each of them one form of the force is greatly predominant. These inrushing forces are alleged to set up on the surface of the "etheric double" [5a] secondary forces at right angles to themselves. The primary force on entrance into the vortex radiates again in straight lines, but at right angles. The number of these radiations of the primal force is said to determine the number of "petals" [6] (as the Hindus call them) which the "Lotus" or vortex exhibits. The secondary force rushing round the vortex produces, it is said, the appearance of the petals of a flower, or, "perhaps more accurately, saucers or shallow vases of wavy iridescent glass". In this way—that is, by supposition of an etheric vortex subject to an incoming

3.—The petals of the lotus are Pranashakti manifested by Pranavayu or vital force. Each lotus is a centre of a different form of "matter" (Bhuta) there predominant—A .A.
4.—This a Western term.—A. A.
5a—b. Not mentioned in the account here given.—A. A.
6.—See last note but three.

154

force of the Logos—both the "Lotuses" described in the Hindu books and the number of their petals is accounted for by the author, who substitutes for the Svadhishthana centre a six-petalled lotus at the spleen, [5b] and corrects the number of petals of the lotus in th head, which he says is not a thousand, as the book of this Yoga say, "but exactly 960". [6a]

"There are some resemblances between this account and the teaching of the Yoga Shastra, with which in a general way the author cited appears to have some acquaintance, and which may have suggested to him some features of his account. There are firstly seven centres, which with one exception correspond with the Chakras described. The author says that there are three other lower centres, but that concentration on them is full of danger. What these are is not stated. There is no centre lower, that I am aware of, than the Muladhara (as the name "root-centre" itself implies), and the only centre near to it which is excluded, in the above-mentioned account, is the Apas Tattva centre, or Svadhishthana. Next there is the Force "the

6a.—So little attention seems to be given to exactitude in this matter that one of the letters is dropped in order to make 1,000 petals—that is 50 x 20. "Thousand" is, here only symbolic of magnitude.—A. A.

Serpent Fire," which the Hindus call Kundalini, in the lowest centre, the Muladhara. Lastly, the effect of the rousing of this force, which is accomplished by will power (Yogabala), [8] is said to exalt the physical consciousness through the ascending planes to the "heaven world". To use the Hindu expression, the object and aim of Shatchakrabheda is Yoga. This is ultimately union with the Supreme Self or Paramatma; but it is obvious, that as the body in its natural state is already, though unconsciously, in Yoga, otherwise it would not exist, each conscious step upwards is Yoga, and there are many stages of such before complete or Kaivalya Mukti is attained. This and, indeed, many of the preceding stages are far beyond the "heaven world" of which the author speaks. Yogis are not concerned with the "heaven world," but seek to surpass it; otherwise they are not Yogis at all. What, according to this theory, manifested force apparently does is this: it enhances the mental and moral qualities of the self-operator as they existed at the time of its discovery. But if this be so, such enhancement may be as little desirable as the original state.

8.—With the aid of bodily purification, certain Asans and Mudras (v. post).

Apart from the necessity for the possession of health and strength, the thought, will, and morality, which it is proposed to subject to its influence must be first purified and strengthened before they are intensified by the vivifying influence of the aroused force. Further, as I have elsewhere pointed out,[9] the Yogis say that the piercing of the Brahmagranthi or "knot"[10] sometimes involves considerable pain, physical dis order, and even disease, as is not unlikely to follow from concentration on such a centre as the navel (Nabhipadma).

"To use Hindu terms, the Sadhaka must be competent (Adhikari), a matter to be determined by his Guru, from whom alone the actual method of Yoga, can be learned. The incidental dangers, however, stated by Mr. Leadbeater go beyond any mentioned to me by Indians themselves, who seem to be in general unaware of the subject of "phallic sorcery", to which reference is made by Mr. Leadbeater, who speaks of schools of (apparently Western) "Black Magic" which are said to use Kundalini for the purpose of stimulating the sexual centre. Another auth-

9.—In the first edition of my Mahanirvana Tantra. CXXIV.
10—There are three "knots" which have to be pierced or centres where the force of Maya is particulary strong.

or says:[11]   "The mere dabbler in the
pseudo-occult will only degrade his intellect
with the puerilities of psychism, become the
prey of the evil influence of the phantasmal
world, or ruin his soul by the foul practices
of phallic sorcery—as thousands of misguid-
ed people are doing even in this age." Is this
so? It is possible that perverse or mis-
guided concentration on sexual and connected centres may have the effect al-
luded to. And it may be that the Commentator Lakshmidara alludes to this
when he speaks of Uttara Kaulas who
arouse Kundalini in the Muladhara
to satisfy their desire for world-enjoy-
ment and do not attempt to lead Her upwards to the Highest Centre which is the object of Yoga seekings super-worldly bliss. Of
such, a Sanskrit verse runs "they are the
true prostitutes". I have, however, never
heard Indians refer to this matter, probably
because, it does not belong to Yoga in its ordinary sense, as also by reason of the antece-
dent discipline required of those who would
undertake this Yoga, the nature of their
practice, and the aim they have in view, such
a possibility does not come under considera-

11.—"The Apocalypse Unsealed," p. 62.

tion. The Indian who practices this or any other kind of spiritual Yoga ordinarily does so not on account of a curious interest in occultism or with a desire to gain "astral" or similar experiences.[12] His attitude in this as in all other matters is essentially a religious one, based on a firm faith in Brahman (Sthiranishtha), and inspired by a desire for union with It which is liberation.

"Assuming for argument the alleged correspondence, then the "etheric centres" or Chakras of Mr. Leadbeater's account appear to be centres of energy of Prana-vayu- or Vital Force. The lotuses are also this and centres of the universal consciousness. Kundalini is the static form of the creative energy in bodies which is the source of all energies, including Prana. According to Mr. Leadbeater's theory, Kundalini is some force which is distinct from Prana, understanding this term to mean vitality of the life-principle, which on entrance into the body shows itself in various manifestations of life which are the minor Pranas, of which inspiration is called by the general name of the

---

12.—Those who do practise magic of the kind mentioned work only in the lowest centre, have recourse to the Prayoga, which leads to Mayika Shiddhi, whereby commerce is had with female spirits and the like. The process in this work described is one upon the path of liberation and has nothing to do with sexual black magic.

force itself (Prana). Verses 10 and 11 says
of Kundalini: "It is She who maintains all
the beings (that is, jiva, jivatma) of the
world by means of inspiration and expira-
tion." She is thus the Prana Devata, but, as
She is (Comm., vv. 10 and 11) Srishti-sthit-
ilayatmika, all forces therefore are in Her.
She is, in fact, the Shabdabrahman or
"Word" in bodies. The theory discussed appears to diverge from that of the Yogis when
we consider the nature of the Chakras and
the question of their vivification. According to Mr. Leadbeater's account, the Chakras are all vortices of "etheric matter", apparently of the same kind and subject to the
same external influence of the inrushing sevenfold force of the "Logos" but differing
in this ,that in each of the Chakras one or
other of their sevenfold forces is predominant. Again, if, as has been stated, the astral
body corresponds with the Manomayako-
sha, then the vivification of the Chakras appears to be, according to Mr. Leadbeater, a
rousing of the Kamik side of the mental
sheath. According to the Hindu doctrine,
these Chakras are differing centres of consciousness, vitality, and Tattvik energy. Each
of the five lower Chakras is the centre of

energy of a gross Tattva–that is, of that form of Tattvik activity or Tanmatra which manifests the Mahabhuta or sensible matter. The sixth is the centre of the subtle mental Tattva, and the Sahasrara is not called a Chakra at all. Nor, as stated, is the splenic centre included among the six Chakras which are dealt with in this account.

"In the Indian system the total number of the petals corresponds with the number of the letters of the Sanskrit Alphabet,[13] and the number of the petals of any specific lotus is determined by the disposition of the subtile "nerves" Nadis around it. These petals, further, bear subtile sound-powers, and are fifty in number, as are the letters of the Sanskrit Alphabet.

"This work also describes certain things which are gained by contemplation on each of the Chakras. Some of them are of general character, such as long life, freedom from desire and sin, control of the senses, knowledge, power of speech, and fame. Some of these and other qualities are results common to concentration on more than one Chakra. Others are stated in connection with the contemplation upon one centre only. Such stat-

13—which are sometimes given as 50 and sometimes as 51.

ments seem to be made, not necessarily with the intention of accurately recording the specific. result, if any, which follows upon concentration upon a particular centre, but by way of praise for increased self-control, or Stuti-vada; as where it is said in v. 21 that contemplation on the Nabhi-padma gains for the Yogi power to destroy and create the world.

"It is also said that mastery of the centres may produce various Siddhis or powers in respect of the predominating elements there. And this is, in fact, alleged. [14] Pandit Ananta Shastri says: [15] "We can meet with several persons every day elbowing us in the streets or bazaars who in all sincerity attempted to reach the highest plane of bliss, but fell victims on the way to the illusions of the psychic world, and stopped at one or the other of the six Chakras. They are of varying degrees of attainment, and are seen to possess some power which is not found even in the best intellectuals of the ordinary run of mankind. That this school of practical psychology was working very well in India at one time is evident from these living ins-

14.—See Yogatattve Upanishad, where contemplation on the earth cen-tre secures mastery over, etc. At the same time it points out that these "powers" are obstacles to liberation.
15.—Anandalahari, p. 35.

tances (not to speak of the numberless treatises on the subject) of men roaming about in all parts of the country." The mere rousing of the Serpent power does not, from the spiritual Yoga standpoint, amount to much. Nothing, however, of real moment, from the higher Yogis' point of view, is achieved until the Ajna Chakra is reached. Here, again, it is said that the Sadhaka whose Atma is nothing but a meditation on this lotus "becomes the creator, preserver, and destroyer, of the three worlds"; and yet, as the commentator points out (v. 34), "This is but the highest Prashangsa-vada or Stutivada—that is, compliment—which in Sanskrit literature is as often void of reality as it is in our ordinary life. Though much is here gained, it is not until the Tattvas of this centre are also absorbed, and complete knowledge [16] of the Sahasrara is gained, that the Yogi attains that which is both his aim and the motive of his labour, cessation from rebirth which follows on the control and concentration of the Chitta on the Shivasthanam, the Abode of Bliss. It is not to be

16.—This, it is obvious, comes only after long effort, and following on less complete experiences and results. According to Indian notions, success (Siddhi) in Yoga may be the fruit of experiences of many preceeding lives. Kundalini must be gradually raised from one centre to another until she reaches the Lotus in the cerebrum. The length of time required varies in the individual—it may be years ordinarily or in exceptional cases months.

supposed that simply because the Serpent
Fire has been aroused that one has thereby
become a Yogi or achieved the end of Yoga.
There are other points of difference which
the reader will discover for himself, but into
which I do not enter, as my object in com-
paring the two accounts has been to estab-
lish a general contrast between this modern
account and that of the Indian schools.   I
may, however, add that the differences are
not only as to details.   The style of thought
differs in a way not easy shortly to describe,
but which will be quickly recognised by
those who have some familiarity with the
Indian Scriptures and mode of thought. The
latter is ever disposed to interpret all proces-
ces and their results from a subjective standpoint, though for the purposes of Sadhana
the objective aspect is not ignored.   The Indian theory is highly philosophical.   Thus,
to take but one instance, whilst Mr. Leadbeater attributes the power of becoming large or small at will (Anima and Mahima
Siddhi) to a flexible tube or "microscopic
snake" in the forehead, the Hindu says that
all powers (Siddhi) are the attributes (Aishvaryya) of the Lord Ishvara, or Creative
Consciousness, and that in the degree that

the Jiva realises that consciousness [17] he shares the powers inherent in the degree of his attainment.

The above is an excerpt from Mr. Avalon's introduction to his book, "The Serpent Power". Every student of Yoga should read it.

17.—As this is by the Devi's grace, She is called "the giver of the eight Siddhis" (Ishitvadyashtasiddhida). See Trishati, II. 47. She gives Aishvaryya.

- F I N I S -

Om, Om, Om.

YOGA VASHISHT OR HEAVEN FOUND

(By the Author)

It is the book for the truth-seekers who are hungry for Spirituality.

It is the guidance for the daily life. The work of the Great Master, who made it so very easy by illustration, that, even a ten year old child can understand it.

This book contains the following chapters:

1—Sri Ram, the Truth Seeker.

2—How Wise should Live.

3—How Suka attained Liberation.

4—The Way to the Blessed State.

5—The Creation of the Universe; Seven States of Wisdom and Seven States of Ignorance.

Read this book and you will never miss the Consciousness of God within you.

- PRICE $3.00 -

For a Limited Time.

In ordering book address:

Rishi Singh Gherwal or J. Falkenstein

P. O. Box 533   Santa Barbara, Calif.

U. S. A.

9 781428 628250